Angular 17 for Juniors: The Basics You Must Know.

CONTENTS

1 INTRODUCTION

Angular is a popular and powerful framework for building web applications. It is developed and maintained by Google and a community of developers and organizations. Angular allows you to create dynamic, interactive, and responsive user interfaces using HTML, CSS, and TypeScript. Angular also provides a rich set of tools and libraries to help you with common tasks such as data binding, routing, testing, and deployment.

Angular 17 is the latest version of Angular, released on November 8, 2023. It introduces some new features and improvements, such as:

- A new branding and documentation site, with a redesigned logo and a more user-friendly and interactive website.
- A new styleUrl property for the @Component decorator, which simplifies the way you link stylesheets to your components.
- A new application builder, which uses vite and esbuild to speed up the development and production processes[2].
- A new built-in syntax for control flow in templates, which allows you to use if, else, and for statements without the need for ngIf and ngFor directives[2].

- A new experimental compiler, which uses the WebAssembly binary format to improve the performance and security of your applications[2].

In this book, you will learn the basics of Angular and how to use it to create web applications. You will also learn how to use the new features and benefits of Angular 17. By the end of this book, you will have a solid understanding of Angular and be able to build your own projects with confidence and ease.

To get started with Angular, you will need to set up your development environment and tools. You will need the following:

- A code editor, such as Visual Studio Code, Atom, or Sublime Text.
- A web browser, such as Chrome, Firefox, or Edge.
- Node.js, which is a JavaScript runtime environment that allows you to run Angular applications on your machine.
- npm, which is a package manager that allows you to install and manage Angular and other dependencies.
- Angular CLI, which is a command-line interface that allows you to create and run Angular projects.

To install Node.js and npm, you can download them from their official website. To install Angular CLI, you can use the following command in your terminal:

npm install -g @angular/cli

To create your first Angular project, you can use the following command in your terminal:

ng new angular-for-juniors

This will create a new folder called angular-for-juniors and generate the files and folders for your project. To run your project in the browser, you can use the following command in your terminal:

ng serve —open

This will start a development server and open your project in your default browser. You should see a welcome message saying "angular-for-juniors app is running!".

Congratulations, you have successfully created and run your first Angular project! In the next chapter, you will learn how to create and use components and templates, which are the building blocks of Angular applications.

But before we move on, let's take a moment to compare Angular with some other technologies that you might have heard of or used before. How does Angular stand out from the crowd? What are the advantages and disadvantages of using Angular over other frameworks or libraries?

Angular vs. React

React is a JavaScript library for building user interfaces. It was created by Facebook and is widely used by many companies and developers. React is based on the concept of components, which are reusable pieces of UI that can have their own state and logic. React also uses a virtual DOM, which is a representation of the real DOM in memory, to optimize the rendering process and avoid unnecessary changes to the DOM.

Some of the main differences between Angular and React are:

- Angular is a complete framework, while React is a library. This means that Angular provides more features and tools out of the box, such as routing, testing, forms, dependency injection, etc. React, on the other hand, requires you to use third-party libraries or tools to achieve the same functionality, such as React Router, Redux, Jest, etc.

- Angular uses TypeScript, while React uses JavaScript. TypeScript is a superset of JavaScript that adds static typing and other features to the language. TypeScript can help you catch errors and bugs at compile time, and provide better tooling and editor support. JavaScript, on the other hand, is more flexible and dynamic, but also more prone to errors and inconsistencies.

- Angular uses templates, while React uses JSX. Templates are HTML files that contain Angular-specific syntax and directives to bind data and events to the components. JSX is a syntax extension that allows you to write HTML-like code in JavaScript files. JSX can make the code more readable and expressive, but also requires a transpiler to convert it to plain JavaScript.

Some of the pros and cons of using Angular over React are:

- Angular is more opinionated and consistent, while React is more flexible and customizable. Angular has a clear and well-defined structure and convention for building applications, which can make the code more organized and maintainable. React, on the other hand, gives you more freedom and choice to use different patterns and architectures, which can make the code more diverse and adaptable.

- Angular is more complex and steep, while React is more simple and easy. Angular has a steeper learning curve and requires more knowledge and skills to master. Angular also has more concepts and features to learn and understand, which can make the development process more challenging and time-consuming. React, on the other hand, has a simpler and easier learning curve and requires less knowledge and skills to get started. React also has fewer concepts and features to learn and understand, which can make the development process more straightforward and fast.

- Angular is more performant and secure, while React is more lightweight and flexible. Angular has a better performance and security than React, thanks to its new application builder and compiler, which use vite, esbuild, and WebAssembly to speed up the development and production processes, and improve the performance and security of the applications. React, on the other hand, has a smaller size and footprint than Angular, thanks to its minimalistic and modular design, which makes it more lightweight and flexible.

Angular vs. Vue.js

Vue.js is a JavaScript framework for building user interfaces. It was created by Evan You and is widely used by many companies and developers. Vue.js is based on the concept of components, which are reusable pieces of UI that can have their own data and logic. Vue.js also uses a virtual DOM, which is a representation of the real DOM in memory, to optimize the rendering process and avoid unnecessary changes to the DOM.

Some of the main differences between Angular and Vue.js are:
- Angular is a complete framework, while Vue.js is a progressive framework. This means that Angular provides more features and tools out of the box, such as routing, testing, forms, dependency injection, etc. Vue.js, on the other hand, allows you to use only the features and tools that you need, and incrementally add more as your application

grows, such as Vue Router, Vuex, Jest, etc.

- Angular uses TypeScript, while Vue.js uses JavaScript. TypeScript is a superset of JavaScript that adds static typing and other features to the language. TypeScript can help you catch errors and bugs at compile time, and provide better tooling and editor support. JavaScript, on the other hand, is more flexible and dynamic, but also more prone to errors and inconsistencies.

- Angular uses templates, while Vue.js uses templates or JSX. Templates are HTML files that contain Angular-specific syntax and directives to bind data and events to the components. JSX is a syntax extension that allows you to write HTML-like code in JavaScript files. JSX can make the code more readable and expressive, but also requires a transpiler to convert it to plain JavaScript. Vue.js gives you the option to use either templates or JSX, depending on your preference and use case.

Some of the pros and cons of using Angular over Vue.js are:

- Angular is more opinionated and consistent, while Vue.js is more flexible and customizable. Angular has a clear and well-defined structure and convention for building applications, which can make the code more organized and maintainable. Vue.js, on the other hand, gives you more freedom and choice to use different patterns and architectures, which can make the code more diverse and adaptable.

- Angular is more complex and steep, while Vue.js is more simple and easy. Angular has a steeper learning curve and requires more knowledge and skills to master. Angular also has more concepts and features to learn and understand, which can make the development process more challenging and time-consuming. Vue.js, on the other hand, has a simpler and easier learning curve and requires less knowledge and skills to get started. Vue.js also has fewer concepts and features to learn and understand, which can make the development process more straightforward and fast.

- Angular is more performant and secure, while Vue.js is more lightweight and flexible. Angular has a better performance and security than Vue.js, thanks to its new application builder and compiler, which use vite, esbuild, and WebAssembly to speed up the development and production processes, and improve the performance and security of the applications. Vue.js, on the other hand, has a smaller size and footprint than Angular, thanks to its minimalistic and modular design, which makes it more lightweight and flexible.

As you can see, Angular has its own strengths and weaknesses compared to other technologies. Depending on your project requirements, preferences, and goals, you might find Angular more suitable or less suitable than other frameworks or libraries. However, one thing is certain: Angular is a powerful and modern framework that can help you create amazing web applications. In this book, we will show you how to do that with Angular 17.

2 COMPONENTS AND TEMPLATES

Components are the building blocks of Angular applications. They are reusable pieces of code that encapsulate the data and logic of a specific part of the user interface. Components are used to create custom elements, which can be used in other parts of the application or in other applications altogether.

To create a component, you need to define a class that contains the data and logic for the component, and a template that defines the structure and appearance of the component. The class and template are then combined to create the component.

Here is an example of a simple component:

```
import { Component } from '@angular/core';

@Component({
selector: 'app-hello-world',
template: '<h1>Hello World!</h1>'
})
export class HelloWorldComponent {}
```

In this example, we define a component called HelloWorldComponent that displays the text "Hello World!" using an HTML heading element. The @Component decorator is used to define the selector and template for the component.

To use this component in another part of the application, you would add the selector to the HTML template:

```
<app-hello-world></app-hello-world>
```

This would render the HelloWorldComponent in the location where the selector is used.

How to use data binding and interpolation

Data binding is a way to connect the data in a component to the template. There are three types of data binding in Angular: property binding, event binding, and two-way binding.

Property binding is used to set the value of an HTML element property to a value in the component. For example, to set the value of an input element to a variable in the component, you would use property binding:

```
<input [value]="name">
```

In this example, the value of the name variable in the component is bound to the value of the input element.

Event binding is used to listen for events in the template and call a function in the component when the event occurs. For example, to call a function in the component when a button is clicked, you would use event binding:

```
<button (click)="doSomething()">Click me!</button>
```

In this example, the doSomething() function in the component is called when the button is clicked.

Two-way binding is used to bind a property in the component to an input element and listen for changes to the input element. For example, to bind the value of an input element to a variable in the component and listen for changes to the input element, you would use two-way binding:

```
<input [(ngModel)]="name">
```

In this example, the value of the name variable in the component is bound to the value of the input element, and changes to the input element are reflected in the name variable.

Interpolation is a way to embed expressions in the template. Expressions are evaluated and the result is displayed in the template. For example, to display the value of a variable in the template, you would use interpolation:

```
<p>{{ name }}</p>
```

In this example, the value of the name variable in the component is displayed in the paragraph element.

How to use directives and pipes

Directives are used to add behavior to HTML elements. There are two types of directives in Angular: structural directives and attribute directives.

Structural directives are used to add or remove elements from the DOM based on conditions. For example, to add an element to the DOM if a condition is true, you would use the *ngIf directive:

```
<div *ngIf="showElement">This element is shown if showElement is
true.</div>
```

In this example, the div element is added to the DOM if the showElement variable in the component is true.

Attribute directives are used to modify the behavior of an HTML element. For example, to change the background color of an element, you would use the ngStyle directive:

```
<div [ngStyle]="{ 'background-color': color }">This element has a
background color of {{ color }}.</div>
```

In this example, the ngStyle directive is used to set the background color of the div element to the value of the color variable in the component.

Pipes are used to transform data in the template. There are several built-in pipes in Angular, such as date, currency, and uppercase. For example, to format a date in the template, you would use the date pipe:

```
<p>The current date is {{ currentDate | date }}</p>
```

In this example, the date pipe is used to format the currentDate variable in the component as a date.

How to use the new control flow syntax

Angular 17 introduces a new syntax for control flow statements in templates. This new syntax is designed to be more concise and easier to read than the previous syntax.

The new syntax includes an @if statement for conditional rendering, an @for statement for looping over arrays, and an @switch statement for switching between different cases.

Here is an example of the new @if statement:

```
<div>
  @if (condition) {
    Content to render when the condition is true.
  } @else {
    Content to render when the condition is false.
  }
</div>
```

In this example, the @if statement is used to conditionally render content based on the value of the condition variable.

Here is an example of the new @for statement:

```
<div>
  @for (let item of items) {
    {{ item }}
  }
</div>
```

In this example, the `@for` statement is used to loop over the `items` array and render each item.

Here is an example of the new `@switch` statement:

```
<div>
  @switch (value) {
    @case 1 {
      Content to render when value is 1.
    }
    @case 2 {
      Content to render when value is 2.
    }
    @default {
      Content to render when value is neither 1 nor 2.
    }
  }
</div>
```

In this example, the @switch statement is used to switch between different cases based on the value of the value variable.

These new control flow statements are designed to make it easier to write and read templates in Angular 17. They are also faster and more efficient than the previous syntax, which should help improve the performance of your applications.

How to use template reference variables and input/output properties

Template reference variables are used to reference elements in the template. They are defined using the # symbol and can be used to reference elements in event handlers and other parts of the template. For example, to reference an input element in the template, you would use a template reference variable:

```
<input #myInput>
<button (click)="doSomething(myInput.value)">Click me!</button>
```

In this example, the #myInput template reference variable is used to reference the input element. The doSomething() function in the component is called when the button is clicked, and the value of the input element is passed as an argument.

Input/output properties are used to pass data between components. Input properties are used to pass data from a parent component to a child component, while output properties are used to pass data from a child component to a parent component. For example, to pass a message from a parent component to a child component, you would use an input property:

```
import { Component, Input } from '@angular/core';

@Component({
   selector: 'app-child',
   template: '<p>{{ message }}</p>'
})
export class ChildComponent {
   @Input() message: string;
}
```

In this example, we define a child component called ChildComponent that displays a message passed to it as an input property. The @Input() decorator is used to define the input property.

To use this component in a parent component, you would pass the message as an input property:

```
<app-child [message]="'Hello from the parent component!'"></app-child>
```

In this example, the message "Hello from the parent component!" is passed to the ChildComponent as an input property. I hope this chapter has been helpful to you. Let me know if you have any other questions!

3 SERVICES AND DEPENDENCY INJECTION

Services and Dependency Injection

Angular is a framework that allows you to create dynamic and interactive web applications. One of the key features of Angular is its **dependency injection** system, which enables you to write modular and testable code. In this chapter, we will learn about **services** and how to use dependency injection to access them in your components.

What are services and how to create them

A service is a class that provides some functionality or data that can be shared across different components. For example, you may have a service that handles logging, authentication, data fetching, or any other common task. A service can also depend on other services, creating a hierarchy of dependencies.

To create a service, you need to use the @Injectable decorator, which tells Angular that this class can be injected into other classes. The @Injectable decorator also accepts a providedIn option, which specifies where the service should be available. The most common option is root, which means that the service is a **singleton** and can be accessed anywhere in the application. For example, let's create a simple service that logs messages to the console:

```
import { Injectable } from '@angular/core';

@Injectable({
  providedIn: 'root'
})
export class LoggerService {
  log(message: string) {
    console.log(message);
  }
}
```

What is dependency injection and how to use it

Dependency injection is a design pattern that allows a class to receive its dependencies from an external source, rather than creating them itself. This makes the class more reusable, testable, and loosely coupled. Angular has a built-in dependency injection system that manages the creation and injection of services and other classes.

To use dependency injection, you need to declare the dependencies of your class in its constructor, using the private or public modifier. Angular will then automatically provide the instances of those dependencies when creating the class. For example, let's create a component that uses the LoggerService we created earlier:

```
import { Component } from '@angular/core';
import { LoggerService } from './logger.service';

@Component({
  selector: 'app-hello',
  template: '<h1>Hello, Angular!</h1>'
})
export class HelloComponent {
  constructor(private logger: LoggerService) {
```

```
    this.logger.log('HelloComponent created');
  }
}
```

Notice how we don't need to create a new instance of LoggerService in the component. Angular will inject it for us, and we can access it using the this.logger property. This way, we can easily swap the LoggerService with a different implementation, or mock it for testing purposes.

How to use providers and injectors

Sometimes, you may want to have more control over how and where a service is provided. For example, you may want to have multiple instances of a service, or provide a different implementation of a service for a specific component. To achieve this, you can use **providers** and **injectors**.

A provider is an object that tells Angular how to create or obtain an instance of a service. A provider can be a class, a value, a factory function, or an alias. You can specify the providers of a service using the providers array in the @Injectable decorator, or in the @NgModule or @Component decorator. For example, let's create a provider that returns a different instance of LoggerService for each component:

```
import { Injectable } from '@angular/core';

@Injectable()
export class LoggerService {
  id: number;

  constructor() {
    this.id = Math.random();
  }
}
```

```
  log(message: string) {
    console.log(`[${this.id}] ${message}`);
  }
}

// In app.module.ts
@NgModule({
  providers: [LoggerService]
})

// In hello.component.ts
@Component({
  selector: 'app-hello',
  template: '<h1>Hello, Angular!</h1>'
})
export class HelloComponent {
  constructor(private logger: LoggerService) {
    this.logger.log('HelloComponent created');
  }
}

// In bye.component.ts
@Component({
  selector: 'app-bye',
  template: '<h1>Bye, Angular!</h1>'
})
export class ByeComponent {
  constructor(private logger: LoggerService) {
    this.logger.log('ByeComponent created');
  }
}
```

Notice how we removed the providedIn option from the @Injectable decorator, and added the LoggerService to the providers array of the @NgModule decorator. This means that the LoggerService will be provided at the module level, and each component that injects it will get a new instance of it. You can verify this by looking at the console and seeing the different ids for each component.

An injector is an object that is responsible for creating and providing instances of services. Angular has a hierarchical injector system, which means that there are multiple injectors at different levels of the application. The root injector is created by the @NgModule decorator, and each component has its own injector that inherits from its parent injector. You can access the injector of a component using the Injector class, which is also injectable. For example, let's create a component that manually requests an instance of LoggerService from its injector:

```
import { Component, Injector } from '@angular/core';
import { LoggerService } from './logger.service';

@Component({
  selector: 'app-manual',
  template: '<h1>Manual Injection</h1>'
})
export class ManualComponent {
  constructor(private injector: Injector) {
    const logger = this.injector.get(LoggerService);
    logger.log('ManualComponent created');
  }
}
```

Notice how we use the injector.get() method to obtain an instance of LoggerService. This is equivalent to declaring the dependency in the constructor, but gives us more flexibility and control over when and how to inject the service.

How to use observables and RxJS

Observables are a powerful way of handling asynchronous and event-based data in Angular. An observable is an object that represents a stream of data that can be observed by one or more subscribers. A subscriber is a function that receives the data emitted by the observable, and can also handle errors and completion events. RxJS is a library that provides many operators and utilities for working with observables.

To create an observable, you can use the Observable class from RxJS, or one of the many creation functions, such as of, from, interval, ajax, etc. To subscribe to an observable, you can use the subscribe method, or the async pipe in the template. For example, let's create a component that displays a counter that increments every second using an observable:

```
import { Component } from '@angular/core';
import { Observable } from 'rxjs';

@Component({
  selector: 'app-counter',
  template: '<h1>Counter: {{counter$ | async}}</h1>'
})
export class CounterComponent {
  counter$: Observable<number>;

  constructor() {
    this.counter$ = new Observable<number>(subscriber => {
      let count = 0;
      setInterval(() => {
        subscriber.next(count++);
      }, 1000);
    });
  }
}
```

otice how we create a new observable using the Observable constructor, and pass a function that receives a subscriber object. The subscriber object has methods to emit data (next), errors (error), and completion (complete) events. In this case, we use the next method to emit the current count every second, using the setInterval function. We then assign the observable to the counter$ property, and use the async pipe in the template to subscribe to it and display the value. The async pipe automatically unsubscribes from the observable when the component is destroyed, preventing memory leaks.

To transform or manipulate the data emitted by an observable, you can use the various operators provided by RxJS, such as map, filter, merge, switchMap, debounceTime, etc. Operators are functions that return a new observable based on the source observable. You can chain multiple operators using the pipe method. For example, let's create a component that displays the current time using an observable and the map operator:

```
import { Component } from '@angular/core';
import { Observable, interval } from 'rxjs';
import { map } from 'rxjs/operators';

@Component({
  selector: 'app-clock',
  template: '<h1>Time: {{time$ | async}}</h1>'
})
export class ClockComponent {
  time$: Observable<string>;

  constructor() {
    this.time$ = interval(1000).pipe(
      map(() => new Date().toLocaleTimeString())
    );
  }
}
```

Notice how we use the interval function to create an observable that emits a number every second, and then use the pipe method to apply the map operator. The map operator takes a function that receives the emitted value and returns a new value. In this case, we use the Date object to get the current time and format it as a string. We then assign the resulting observable to the time$ property, and use the async pipe in the template to subscribe to it and display the value.

Observables are very useful for handling user interactions, such as clicks, inputs, scrolls, etc. You can use the fromEvent function to create an observable from any DOM event. The fromEvent function takes an element and an event name as arguments, and returns an observable that emits the event object whenever the event occurs. For example, let's create a component that displays the mouse coordinates using an observable and the fromEvent function:

```
import { Component, OnInit, OnDestroy } from '@angular/core';
import { fromEvent, Subscription } from 'rxjs';

@Component({
  selector: 'app-mouse',
  template: '<h1>Mouse: {{x}}, {{y}}</h1>'
})
export class MouseComponent implements OnInit, OnDestroy {
  x: number;
  y: number;
  subscription: Subscription;

  constructor() {
    this.x = 0;
    this.y = 0;
  }

  ngOnInit() {
    const mouse$ = fromEvent(document, 'mousemove');
    this.subscription = mouse$.subscribe(event => {
      this.x = event.clientX;
      this.y = event.clientY;
    });
  }

  ngOnDestroy() {
    this.subscription.unsubscribe();
```

```
    }
  }
```

Notice how we use the fromEvent function to create an observable from the mousemove event on the document element, and then subscribe to it in the ngOnInit lifecycle hook. The subscription object allows us to unsubscribe from the observable in the ngOnDestroy lifecycle hook, preventing memory leaks. We then update the x and y properties with the mouse coordinates from the event object, and display them in the template.

Observables are also very useful for communicating data between components, especially when they are not directly related. You can use a service to create and share an observable, and then inject the service into the components that need to access the data. For example, let's create a service that emits a random number every second using an observable, and then use it in two components:

```
import { Injectable } from '@angular/core';
import { Observable, interval } from 'rxjs';
import { map } from 'rxjs/operators';

@Injectable({
  providedIn: 'root'
})
export class RandomService {
  random$: Observable<number>;

  constructor() {
    this.random$ = interval(1000).pipe(
      map(() => Math.floor(Math.random() * 100))
    );
  }
}
```

```
// In app.component.ts
import { Component } from '@angular/core';
import { RandomService } from './random.service';

@Component({
  selector: 'app-root',
  template: '<app-display></app-display><app-square></app-square>'
})
export class AppComponent {
  constructor(private random: RandomService) {
    this.random.random$.subscribe(value => {
      console.log(`App: ${value}`);
    });
  }
}

// In display.component.ts
import { Component } from '@angular/core';
import { RandomService } from './random.service';

@Component({
  selector: 'app-display',
  template: '<h1>Display: {{random.random$ | async}}</h1>'
})
export class DisplayComponent {
  constructor(public random: RandomService) {}
}

// In square.component.ts
import { Component } from '@angular/core';
import { RandomService } from './random.service';

@Component({
  selector: 'app-square',
  template: '<h1>Square: {{square$ | async}}</h1>'
})
export class SquareComponent {
  square$: Observable<number>;
```

```
constructor(private random: RandomService) {
  this.square$ = this.random.random$.pipe(
    map(value => value * value)
  );
}
}
```

Notice how we create a service that provides an observable that emits a random number every second, and then inject it into the AppComponent, the DisplayComponent, and the SquareComponent. The AppComponent subscribes to the observable and logs the value to the console. The DisplayComponent uses the async pipe to subscribe to the observable and display the value in the template. The SquareComponent uses the pipe method to apply the map operator to the observable, and then uses the async pipe to subscribe to the resulting observable and display the square of the value in the template. This way, we can share data between components using observables and services.

This concludes the chapter on services and dependency injection. In this chapter, we learned about:

- What are services and how to create them using the @Injectable decorator
- What is dependency injection and how to use it to access services in components
- How to use providers and injectors to control the scope and availability of services
- How to use observables and RxJS to handle asynchronous and event-based data
- How to create, transform, and subscribe to observables using various functions and operators
- How to communicate data between components using observables and services

We hope you enjoyed this chapter and learned something new. In the next chapter, we will explore the topic of routing and navigation in Angular.

4 ROUTING AND NAVIGATION

Angular is a framework that allows you to create single-page applications, which means that the entire application is loaded in one page, and the content is dynamically updated without refreshing the page. One of the challenges of single-page applications is how to handle the navigation and URL changes, which are essential for user experience and SEO. Angular solves this problem by providing a **routing** system, which enables you to define the paths and components for different views of your application, and to navigate between them using links, buttons, or programmatic logic.

In this chapter, we will learn about routing and navigation in Angular. We will cover the following topics:

- What is routing and how to configure it using the RouterModule and the Routes array
- How to use router outlets and links to display and navigate to different views
- How to use route parameters and query parameters to pass data to the components
- How to use guards and resolvers to protect and preload the routes
- How to use the View Transitions API to animate the transitions between the views

What is routing and how to configure it

Routing is the process of mapping a URL to a component, and vice versa. Routing allows you to create multiple views for your application, and to switch between them based on the URL. Routing also enables you to use the browser's history and bookmarks features, and to support deep linking and SEO.

To use routing in Angular, you need to import the RouterModule from @angular/router, and configure it with a Routes array, which is an array of objects that define the routes of your application. Each route object has a path property, which is a string that matches the URL, and a component property, which is a class that represents the component to be displayed for that path. Optionally, you can also specify other properties, such as redirectTo, children, canActivate, resolve, etc., which we will discuss later. For example, let's create a simple routing configuration for an application that has three components: HomeComponent, AboutComponent, and ContactComponent:

```
import { NgModule } from '@angular/core';
import { RouterModule, Routes } from '@angular/router';
import { HomeComponent } from './home.component';
import { AboutComponent } from './about.component';
import { ContactComponent } from './contact.component';

const routes: Routes = [
  { path: '', component: HomeComponent },
  { path: 'about', component: AboutComponent },
  { path: 'contact', component: ContactComponent }
];

@NgModule({
  imports: [RouterModule.forRoot(routes)],
  exports: [RouterModule]
})
```

```
export class AppRoutingModule {}
```

Notice how we import the RouterModule and the Routes type from @angular/router, and the components from their respective files. We then create a routes array, and define three routes: one for the empty path (''), which corresponds to the root URL (/), and one for each of the about and contact paths, which correspond to the /about and /contact URLs. We then use the RouterModule.forRoot() method to create a module with the routing configuration, and export the RouterModule so that it can be imported by other modules. We also create a class called AppRoutingModule to represent the routing module, which we will import in the AppModule.

To enable routing in your application, you need to import the AppRoutingModule in the AppModule, and add it to the imports array. For example:

```
import { NgModule } from '@angular/core';
import { BrowserModule } from '@angular/platform-browser';
import { AppComponent } from './app.component';
import { AppRoutingModule } from './app-routing.module';
import { HomeComponent } from './home.component';
import { AboutComponent } from './about.component';
import { ContactComponent } from './contact.component';

@NgModule({
  declarations: [AppComponent, HomeComponent, AboutComponent,
ContactComponent],
  imports: [BrowserModule, AppRoutingModule],
  bootstrap: [AppComponent]
})
export class AppModule {}
```

Notice how we import the AppRoutingModule and the components from their respective files, and add them to the imports and declarations arrays. We also import the BrowserModule, which provides the essential services for running the application in the browser, and the AppComponent, which is the root component of the application. We then use the @NgModule decorator to create a module with the configuration, and export the AppModule class to represent the module.

How to use router outlets and links

Now that we have configured the routing for our application, we need to tell Angular where and how to display the components for each route. To do this, we use two directives: <router-outlet> and <a routerLink>.

The <router-outlet> directive is a placeholder that marks the location where the component for the current route should be rendered. You can place the <router-outlet> directive anywhere in your template, but typically you would put it in the root component, or in a layout component that contains the common elements of your application, such as the header, footer, sidebar, etc. For example, let's create a simple template for the AppComponent that has a <router-outlet> directive:

```
<h1>My Angular App</h1>
<nav>
  <a routerLink="/">Home</a>
  <a routerLink="/about">About</a>
  <a routerLink="/contact">Contact</a>
</nav>
<router-outlet></router-outlet>
```

Notice how we use the <router-outlet> directive to indicate where the component for the current route should be displayed. We also use the <a routerLink> directive to create links that navigate to the different routes. The routerLink directive is an attribute that takes a string or an array that represents the path to the route. The routerLink directive also adds some classes to the link element, such as router-link-active, which indicates that the link corresponds to the current route. You can use these classes to style the links accordingly.

When the application is loaded, Angular will look at the URL and match it with the path property of the routes array. If it finds a match, it will create an instance of the component specified by the component property of the route object, and render it in the <router-outlet> directive. If it does not find a match, it will display an empty view. For example, if the URL is /, Angular will render the HomeComponent in the <router-outlet> directive. If the URL is /about, Angular will render the AboutComponent in the <router-outlet> directive. If the URL is /contact, Angular will render the ContactComponent in the <router-outlet> directive. If the URL is /foo, Angular will display an empty view, since there is no route for that path.

You can also navigate to the different routes programmatically, using the Router service, which is injectable in any component. The Router service has a navigate method, which takes an array that represents the path to the route, and optionally a NavigationExtras object, which contains additional options, such as queryParams, fragment, replaceUrl, etc. For example, let's create a button in the HomeComponent that navigates to the AboutComponent:

```
import { Component } from '@angular/core';
import { Router } from '@angular/router';

@Component({
  selector: 'app-home',
  template: '<h2>Home</h2><button (click)="goToAbout()">Go to
About</button>'
})
export class HomeComponent {
  constructor(private router: Router) {}

  goToAbout() {
```

```
    this.router.navigate(['/about']);
  }
}
```

Notice how we inject the Router service in the constructor, and use the navigate method to navigate to the /about path when the button is clicked. We can also pass a second argument to the navigate method, which is an object that contains additional options, such as queryParams, which are key-value pairs that are appended to the URL after a ? symbol, and fragment, which is a string that is appended to the URL after a # symbol. For example, let's modify the goToAbout method to pass some query parameters and a fragment:

```
goToAbout() {
    this.router.navigate(['/about'], {
        queryParams: { name: 'Alice', age: 25 },
        fragment: 'bio'
    });
  }
```

This will navigate to the /about?name=Alice&age=25#bio URL, which can be used to pass some data or state to the AboutComponent.

How to use route parameters and query parameters

Sometimes, you may want to have dynamic routes that depend on some data or input from the user. For example, you may have a route that displays the details of a product, and the product id is part of the URL. To achieve this, you can use **route parameters** and **query parameters**.

Route parameters are segments of the URL that are prefixed with a : symbol, and represent a variable that can change depending on the data. Route parameters are part of the path property of the route object, and can be accessed in the component using the ActivatedRoute service, which is injectable in any component. The ActivatedRoute service has a params property, which is an observable that emits the route parameters as an object. For example, let's create a route that displays the details of a product, and the product id is part of the URL:

```
import { NgModule } from '@angular/core';
import { RouterModule, Routes } from '@angular/router';
import { ProductListComponent } from './product-list.component';
import { ProductDetailComponent } from './product-detail.component';

const routes: Routes = [
  { path: 'products', component: ProductListComponent },
  { path: 'products/:id', component: ProductDetailComponent }
];

@NgModule({
  imports: [RouterModule.forRoot(routes)],
  exports: [RouterModule]
})
export class AppRoutingModule {}
```

Notice how we use the :id segment in the path property of the second route, which represents the product id. We then create a ProductDetailComponent that displays the details of the product based on the id. To access the id in the component, we inject the ActivatedRoute service in the constructor, and subscribe to the params observable. For example:

```
import { Component, OnInit } from '@angular/core';
import { ActivatedRoute } from '@angular/router';
import { ProductService } from './product.service';
import { Product } from './product.model';

@Component({
  selector: 'app-product-detail',
  template: `
```

```
<h2>Product Detail</h2>
<div *ngIf="product">
  <p>Name: {{product.name}}</p>
  <p>Price: {{product.price}}</p>
  <p>Description: {{product.description}}</p>
</div>


})
export class ProductDetailComponent implements OnInit {
  product: Product;

  constructor(
    private route: ActivatedRoute,
    private productService: ProductService
  ) {}

  ngOnInit() {
    this.route.params.subscribe(params => {
      const id = +params['id']; // the + operator converts the
string to a number
      this.product = this.productService.getProductById(id);
    });
  }
}
```

Notice how we use the route.params observable to get the route parameters as an object, and then extract the id property from it. We then use the productService to get the product by id, and assign it to the product property, which is displayed in the template.

Query parameters are key-value pairs that are appended to the URL after a ? symbol, and represent some optional data or state that can be passed to the component. Query parameters are not part of the path property of the route object, and can be accessed in the component using the ActivatedRoute service, which has a queryParams property, which is an observable that emits the query parameters as an object. For example, let's modify the ProductListComponent to have a search input that filters the products by name, and passes the search term as a query parameter to the ProductDetailComponent:

```
import { Component } from '@angular/core';
import { Router } from '@angular/router';
import { ProductService } from './product.service';
import { Product } from './product.model';

@Component({
  selector: 'app-product-list',
  template: `
    <h2>Product List</h2>
    <input type="text" [(ngModel)]="search" placeholder="Search by
name" />
    <ul>
      <li *ngFor="let product of filteredProducts">
        <a
          [routerLink]="['/products', product.id]"
          [queryParams]="{ search: search }"
          >{{product.name}}</a
        >
      </li>
    </ul>
  `
})
export class ProductListComponent {
  products: Product[];
  search: string;

  constructor(private router: Router, private productService:
ProductService) {
    this.products = this.productService.getProducts();
    this.search = '';
  }

  get filteredProducts() {
    return this.products.filter(product =>
      product.name.toLowerCase().includes(this.search.toLowerCase())
```

```
    );
  }
}
```

Notice how we use the [(ngModel)] directive to bind the input value to the search property, and use the filteredProducts getter to filter the products by name. We then use the [routerLink] directive to create a link to the ProductDetailComponent, and pass the search property as a query parameter using the [queryParams] directive. This will append the ?search=... to the URL when the link is clicked.

To access the query parameters in the ProductDetailComponent, we inject the ActivatedRoute service in the constructor, and subscribe to the queryParams observable. For example, let's modify the ProductDetailComponent to display the search term as well:

```
import { Component, OnInit } from '@angular/core';
import { ActivatedRoute } from '@angular/router';
import { ProductService } from './product.service';
import { Product } from './product.model';

@Component({
  selector: 'app-product-detail',
  template: `
    <h2>Product Detail</h2>
    <div *ngIf="product">
      <p>Name: {{product.name}}</p>
      <p>Price: {{product.price}}</p>
      <p>Description: {{product.description}}</p>
      <p *ngIf="search">Search term: {{search}}</p>
    </div>
  `
})
export class ProductDetailComponent implements OnInit {
  product: Product;
  search: string;
```

```
constructor(
  private route: ActivatedRoute,
  private productService: ProductService
) {}

ngOnInit() {
  this.route.params.subscribe(params => {
    const id = +params['id'];
    this.product = this.productService.getProductById(id);
  });
  this.route.queryParams.subscribe(queryParams => {
    this.search = queryParams['search'];
  });
}
}
```

Notice how we use the route.queryParams observable to get the query parameters as an object, and then extract the search property from it. We then assign it to the search property, which is displayed in the template if it exists.

How to use guards and resolvers

Sometimes, you may want to have some logic or conditions that determine whether a route can be activated or deactivated, or whether some data needs to be fetched before activating a route. For example, you may want to prevent unauthorized users from accessing some routes, or you may want to load some data from a server before displaying a component. To achieve this, you can use **guards** and **resolvers**.

Guards are classes that implement one of the following interfaces: CanActivate, CanActivateChild, CanDeactivate, or CanLoad. Guards are used to check whether a route can be activated or deactivated, based on some logic or condition. Guards can return a boolean, an observable that emits a boolean, or a promise that resolves to a boolean. Guards can also navigate to a different route or display an error message, if the condition is not met. Guards are specified in the canActivate, canActivateChild, canDeactivate, or canLoad property of the route object, and can be injected in any component. For example, let's create a guard that checks whether the user is logged in before activating a route:

```
import { Injectable } from '@angular/core';
import { CanActivate, Router, ActivatedRouteSnapshot,
RouterStateSnapshot } from '@angular/router';
import { AuthService } from './auth.service';

@Injectable({
  providedIn: 'root'
})
export class AuthGuard implements CanActivate {
  constructor(private router: Router, private authService:
AuthService) {}

  canActivate(route: ActivatedRouteSnapshot, state:
RouterStateSnapshot) {
    if (this.authService.isLoggedIn()) {
      return true;
    } else {
      this.router.navigate(['/login'], {
        queryParams: { returnUrl: state.url }
      });
      return false;
    }
  }
}
```

Notice how we implement the CanActivate interface, and inject the Router and AuthService services in the constructor. The AuthService is a service that handles the authentication logic, and has a isLoggedIn method that returns a boolean indicating whether the user is logged in or not. The canActivate method takes two arguments: route, which is the current route, and state, which is the current state of the router. The canActivate method checks whether the user is logged in, and returns true if so, or false otherwise. If the user is not logged in, the canActivate method also navigates to the /login route, and passes the original URL as a query parameter, so that the user can be redirected back after logging in.

To use the guard, we need to specify it in the canActivate property of the route object that we want to protect. For example, let's create a route that displays the user profile, and use the AuthGuard to protect it:

```
import { NgModule } from '@angular/core';
import { RouterModule, Routes } from '@angular/router';
import { ProfileComponent } from './profile.component';
import { AuthGuard } from './auth.guard';

const routes: Routes = [
  { path: 'profile', component: ProfileComponent, canActivate:
[AuthGuard] }
];

@NgModule({
  imports: [RouterModule.forRoot(routes)],
  exports: [RouterModule]
})
export class AppRoutingModule {}
```

Notice how we import the ProfileComponent and the AuthGuard from their respective files, and add the AuthGuard to the canActivate array of the route object. This means that the ProfileComponent will only be displayed if the user is logged in, otherwise the user will be redirected to the /login route.

Resolvers are classes that implement the Resolve interface, which has a resolve method that returns some data or an observable that emits some data. Resolvers are used to fetch some data from a server or a service before activating a route, and pass it to the component as an input. Resolvers can also handle errors or loading indicators, if the data fetching is slow or fails. Resolvers are specified in the resolve property of the route object, and can be injected in any component. For example, let's create a resolver that fetches the product details from a server before activating the ProductDetailComponent:

```
import { Injectable } from '@angular/core';
import { Resolve, ActivatedRouteSnapshot, RouterStateSnapshot } from
'@angular/router';
import { Observable } from 'rxjs';
import { ProductService } from './product.service';
import { Product } from './product.model';

@Injectable({
  providedIn: 'root'
})
export class ProductResolver implements Resolve<Product> {
  constructor(private productService: ProductService) {}

  resolve(route: ActivatedRouteSnapshot, state: RouterStateSnapshot):
Observable<Product> {
    const id = +route.params['id'];
    return this.productService.getProductById(id);
  }
}
```

Notice how we implement the Resolve<Product> interface, and inject the ProductService in the constructor. The ProductService is a service that handles the communication with the server, and has a getProductById method that returns an observable that emits the product details. The resolve method takes two arguments: route, which is the current route, and state, which is the current state of the router. The resolve method extracts the id parameter from the route, and returns the observable from the getProductById method.

To use the resolver, we need to specify it in the resolve property of the route object that we want to preload. For example, let's modify the route for the ProductDetailComponent to use the ProductResolver:

```
import { NgModule } from '@angular/core';
import { RouterModule, Routes } from '@angular/router';
import { ProductListComponent } from './product-list.component';
import { ProductDetailComponent } from './product-detail.component';
import { ProductResolver } from './product.resolver';

const routes: Routes = [
  { path: 'products', component: ProductListComponent },
  {
    path: 'products/:id',
    component: ProductDetailComponent,
    resolve: { product: ProductResolver }
  }
];

@NgModule({
  imports: [RouterModule.forRoot(routes)],
  exports: [RouterModule]
})
export class AppRoutingModule {}
```

Notice how we import the ProductResolver from its file, and add it to the resolve object of the route object, with a key of product. This means that the ProductResolver will be invoked before activating the route, and the resolved data will be available as an input to the component with the key of product.

To access the resolved data in the ProductDetailComponent, we inject the ActivatedRoute service in the constructor, and use the data property, which is an observable that emits the resolved data as an object. For example, let's modify the ProductDetailComponent to use the resolved data:

```
import { Component, OnInit } from '@angular/core';
import { ActivatedRoute } from '@angular/router';
import { Product } from './product.model';

@Component({
  selector: 'app-product-detail',
  template: `
    <h2>Product Detail</h2>
    <div *ngIf="product">
      <p>Name: {{product.name}}</p>
      <p>Price: {{product.price}}</p>
      <p>Description: {{product.description}}</p>
    </div>
  `
})
export class ProductDetailComponent implements OnInit {
  product: Product;

  constructor(private route: ActivatedRoute) {}

  ngOnInit() {
    this.route.data.subscribe(data => {
      this.product = data['product'];
    });
  }
}
```

Notice how we use the route.data observable to get the resolved data as an object, and then extract the product property from it. We then assign it to the product property, which is displayed in the template.

How to use the View Transitions API

The View Transitions API is a feature of Angular that allows you to animate the transitions between the views, using the @angular/animations module. The View Transitions API provides a declarative way of defining animations, using the @Component decorator and the animations and transition properties. The View Transitions API also integrates with the routing system, using the @route.animations directive and the animation property of the route object. For example, let's create a simple animation that fades in and out the components when the route changes:

```typescript
import { NgModule } from '@angular/core';
import { RouterModule, Routes } from '@angular/router';
import { BrowserAnimationsModule } from '@angular/platform-
browser/animations';
import { HomeComponent } from './home.component';
import { AboutComponent } from './about.component';
import { ContactComponent } from './contact.component';
import { trigger, state, style, animate, transition } from
'@angular/animations';

const routes: Routes = [
  { path: '', component: HomeComponent, data: { animation: 'home' }
},
  { path: 'about', component: AboutComponent, data: { animation:
'about' } },
  { path: 'contact', component: ContactComponent, data: { animation:
'contact' } }
];

@NgModule({
  imports: [RouterModule.forRoot(routes), BrowserAnimationsModule],
  exports: [RouterModule]
})
export class AppRoutingModule {}

// In app.component.ts
import { Component } from '@angular/core';
```

```
import { RouterOutlet } from '@angular/router';
import { trigger, state, style, animate, transition } from
'@angular/animations';

@Component({
  selector: 'app-root',
  template: `
    <h1>My Angular App</h1>
    <nav>
      <a routerLink="/">Home</a>
      <a routerLink="/about">About</a>
      <a routerLink="/contact">Contact</a>
    </nav>
    <div [@route.animations]="prepareRoute(outlet)">
      <router-outlet #outlet="outlet"></router-outlet>
    </div>
  `,
  animations: [
    trigger('route.animations', [
      transition('home => about, home => contact, about => contact',
[
        style({ position: 'relative' }),
        query(':enter, :leave', [
          style({
            position: 'absolute',
            top: 0,
            left: 0,
            width: '100%'
          })
        ]),
        query(':enter', [style({ opacity: 0 })]),
        query(':leave', [animate('500ms ease-out', style({ opacity: 0
}))]),
        query(':enter', [animate('500ms ease-out', style({ opacity: 1
}))])
      ]),
      transition('contact => about, contact => home, about => home',
[
        style({ position: 'relative' }),
        query(':enter, :leave', [
```

```
        style({
          position: 'absolute',
          top: 0,
          right: 0,
          width: '100%'
        })
      ]),
      query(':enter', [style({ opacity: 0 })]),
      query(':leave', [animate('500ms ease-out', style({ opacity: 0
})])]),
      query(':enter', [animate('500ms ease-out', style({ opacity: 1
})])])
    ])
  ])
]
})
export class AppComponent {
  prepareRoute(outlet: RouterOutlet) {
    return outlet && outlet.activatedRouteData &&
outlet.activatedRouteData.animation;
  }
}
```

Notice how we import the BrowserAnimationsModule and the animation functions from @angular/animations, and add them to the imports and animations arrays. We also add a data property to each route object, with an animation property that specifies a unique name for the route. We then use the @route.animations directive in the template, and bind it to a prepareRoute method that returns the animation name based on the current route. We also use the #outlet template reference variable to access the RouterOutlet instance. We then define a trigger function with the name of route.animations, and pass an array of transition functions that specify the animation logic for each route change. The transition function takes a string that represents the direction of the route change, and an array of animation steps that use the style, query, animate functions to manipulate the elements. In this case, we use the query function to select the entering and leaving components, and apply some styles and animations to them. We also use the position property to make the components overlap, and the opacity property to make them fade in and out. The result is a simple fade animation that transitions between the views.

This concludes the chapter on routing and navigation. In this chapter, we learned about:

- What is routing and how to configure it using the RouterModule and the Routes array
- How to use router outlets and links to display and navigate to different views
- How to use route parameters and query parameters to pass data to the components
- How to use guards and resolvers to protect and preload the routes
- How to use the View Transitions API to animate the transitions between the views

We hope you enjoyed this chapter and learned something new. In the next chapter, we will explore the topic of forms and validation in Angular.

5 FORMS AND VALIDATION

Forms are one of the most common features of web applications, as they allow users to enter and submit data, such as login credentials, personal information, preferences, orders, etc. Forms are also one of the most challenging features to implement, as they require a lot of logic and validation to ensure that the data is correct, complete, and secure. Angular provides a powerful and flexible way of creating and managing forms, using the @angular/forms module. Angular supports two types of forms: **template-driven** and **reactive**.

In this chapter, we will learn about forms and validation in Angular. We will cover the following topics:

- What are forms and how to use them using the FormsModule and the ReactiveFormsModule
- How to use template-driven forms and the ngModel and ngForm directives
- How to use reactive forms and the FormControl, FormGroup, and FormArray classes
- How to use form controls and form groups to create and manipulate form fields
- How to use validators and custom validators to validate form fields and display error

messages
- How to use dynamic forms and form arrays to create and manage forms dynamically

What are forms and how to use them

Forms are a way of collecting and submitting data from the user. Forms consist of form fields, which are the individual elements that allow the user to enter or select data, such as input, select, checkbox, radio, etc. Forms also have a submit button, which triggers the submission of the form data to the server or some other logic. Forms can have different states, such as valid, invalid, dirty, pristine, touched, untouched, etc., which indicate the status and quality of the form data.

To use forms in Angular, you need to import the FormsModule or the ReactiveFormsModule from @angular/forms, depending on the type of form you want to create. The FormsModule enables the template-driven approach, which allows you to create and manage forms using HTML templates and directives. The ReactiveFormsModule enables the reactive approach, which allows you to create and manage forms using code and classes. You can also use both modules in the same application, if you need to use both types of forms.

To enable forms in your application, you need to import the FormsModule or the ReactiveFormsModule in the AppModule, and add it to the imports array. For example:

```
import { NgModule } from '@angular/core';
import { BrowserModule } from '@angular/platform-browser';
import { FormsModule, ReactiveFormsModule } from '@angular/forms';
import { AppComponent } from './app.component';

@NgModule({
  declarations: [AppComponent],
  imports: [BrowserModule, FormsModule, ReactiveFormsModule],
  bootstrap: [AppComponent]
```

```
})
export class AppModule {}
```

Notice how we import the FormsModule and the ReactiveFormsModule from @angular/forms, and add them to the imports array. We also import the BrowserModule, which provides the essential services for running the application in the browser, and the AppComponent, which is the root component of the application. We then use the @NgModule decorator to create a module with the configuration, and export the AppModule class to represent the module.

How to use template-driven forms

Template-driven forms are a way of creating and managing forms using HTML templates and directives. Template-driven forms are easy to use and understand, as they rely on the familiar HTML syntax and attributes. Template-driven forms are suitable for simple and static forms, where the form structure and logic are not too complex or dynamic.

To create a template-driven form, you need to use the <form> element, and add the ngForm directive to it. The ngForm directive is a built-in directive that creates and controls a FormGroup instance, which is a class that represents a group of form fields. The ngForm directive also provides some properties and methods to access and manipulate the form data and state, such as value, valid, dirty, reset, etc.

To create a form field, you need to use an input element, such as <input>, <select>, <textarea>, etc., and add the ngModel directive to it. The ngModel directive is a built-in directive that creates and controls a FormControl instance, which is a class that represents a single form field. The ngModel directive also binds the input element to a property of the component class, using the [(ngModel)] syntax, which is a shorthand for the ngModel input and output properties. The ngModel directive also provides some properties and methods to access and manipulate the form field data and state, such as value, valid, dirty, reset, etc.

To submit a template-driven form, you need to use a button element, and add the type="submit" attribute to it. You also need to add the (ngSubmit) output property to the <form> element, and bind it to a method of the component class, which will handle the form submission logic. The (ngSubmit) event will only be emitted if the form is valid, otherwise it will be prevented. You can also access the ngForm instance using the #form template reference variable, which can be passed as an argument to the submission method. For example, let's create a simple template-driven form that collects the user's name and email, and displays them on the console when the form is submitted:

```
<form #form="ngForm" (ngSubmit)="onSubmit(form)">
  <div>
    <label for="name">Name:</label>
    <input id="name" type="text" name="name" [(ngModel)]="user.name"
/>
  </div>
  <div>
    <label for="email">Email:</label>
    <input id="email" type="email" name="email"
[(ngModel)]="user.email" />
  </div>
  <button type="submit">Submit</button>
</form>
```

```
import { Component } from '@angular/core';
import { NgForm } from '@angular/forms';

@Component({
  selector: 'app-root',
  templateUrl: './app.component.html'
```

```
})
export class AppComponent {
  user = {
    name: '',
    email: ''
  };

  onSubmit(form: NgForm) {
    console.log(form.value);
  }
}
```

Notice how we use the <form> element with the ngForm directive and the (ngSubmit) output property, and bind it to the onSubmit method of the component class. We also use the #form template reference variable to access the ngForm instance, and pass it as an argument to the onSubmit method. We then use the <input> elements with the ngModel directive and the [(ngModel)] syntax, and bind them to the user.name and user.email properties of the component class. We also use the name attribute to give a name to each form field, which is required for the ngModel directive to work. We then use the <button> element with the type="submit" attribute to trigger the form submission. In the component class, we define a user object that holds the initial values of the form fields, and a onSubmit method that logs the form value to the console.

How to use reactive forms

Reactive forms are a way of creating and managing forms using code and classes. Reactive forms are more powerful and flexible than template-driven forms, as they allow you to create and manipulate forms dynamically, using reactive programming principles and operators. Reactive forms are suitable for complex and dynamic forms, where the form structure and logic are too complicated or variable to be expressed in HTML templates.

To create a reactive form, you need to use the FormGroup and FormControl classes, which are imported from @angular/forms. The FormGroup class represents a group of form fields, and the FormControl class represents a single form field. You can create and initialize a FormGroup instance with an object that maps the names of the form fields to the FormControl instances, using the new keyword or the formBuilder service, which is a helper service that simplifies the creation of forms. You can also nest FormGroup instances within each other, to create more complex forms.

To display a reactive form, you need to use the <form> element, and add the [formGroup] input property to it, and bind it to the FormGroup instance. You also need to use the input elements, such as <input>, <select>, <textarea>, etc., and add the [formControlName] input property to them, and bind it to the name of the FormControl instance. You can also use the <div> element with the [formGroupName] input property, to create nested form groups.

To submit a reactive form, you need to use a button element, and add the type="submit" attribute to it. You also need to add the (ngSubmit) output property to the <form> element, and bind it to a method of the component class, which will handle the form submission logic. The (ngSubmit) event will only be emitted if the form is valid, otherwise it will be prevented. You can also access the FormGroup instance using the #form template reference variable, which can be passed as an argument to the submission method. For example, let's create a simple reactive form that collects the user's name and email, and displays them on the console when the form is submitted:

```
import { Component, OnInit } from '@angular/core';
import { FormGroup, FormControl } from '@angular/forms';

@Component({
  selector: 'app-root',
```

```
  template: `
    <form [formGroup]="form" #form="ngForm"
(ngSubmit)="onSubmit(form)">
      <div>
        <label for="name">Name:</label>
        <input id="name" type="text" formControlName="name" />
      </div>
      <div>
        <label for="email">Email:</label>
        <input id="email" type="email" formControlName="email" />
      </div>
      <button type="submit">Submit</button>
    </form>
    `
})
export class AppComponent implements OnInit {
  form: FormGroup;

  ngOnInit() {
    this.form = new FormGroup({
      name: new FormControl(''),
      email: new FormControl('')
    });
  }

  onSubmit(form: FormGroup) {
    console.log(form.value);
  }
}
```

Notice how we use the FormGroup and FormControl classes to create and initialize the form property, which holds the form data and state. We then use the [formGroup] input property to bind the <form> element to the form property, and the [formControlName] input property to bind the <input> elements to the name and email properties. We also use the #form template reference variable to access the FormGroup instance, and pass it as an argument to the onSubmit method. We then use the <button> element with the type="submit" attribute to trigger the form submission. In the component class, we define a onSubmit method that logs the form value to the console.

How to use form controls and form groups

Form controls and form groups are the building blocks of reactive forms. Form controls represent individual form fields, and form groups represent collections of form fields. Form controls and form groups have properties and methods that allow you to access and manipulate the form data and state, such as value, setValue, patchValue, valid, invalid, dirty, pristine, touched, untouched, errors, reset , etc.

Form controls and form groups can be created and initialized using the new keyword or the formBuilder service. The formBuilder service is a helper service that simplifies the creation of forms, using a factory method for each type of form model. The formBuilder service has three methods: control, group, and array, which create a FormControl, a FormGroup, and a FormArray respectively. The FormArray class is a subclass of FormGroup that represents an array of form controls or form groups, which we will discuss later.

To use the formBuilder service, you need to inject it in the constructor of the component class, and use it in the ngOnInit lifecycle hook to create and initialize the form model. For example, let's rewrite the previous example using the formBuilder service:

```
import { Component, OnInit } from '@angular/core';
import { FormGroup, FormBuilder } from '@angular/forms';

@Component({
  selector: 'app-root',
  template: `
```

```
    <form [formGroup]="form" #form="ngForm"
(ngSubmit)="onSubmit(form)">
      <div>
        <label for="name">Name:</label>
        <input id="name" type="text" formControlName="name" />
      </div>
      <div>
        <label for="email">Email:</label>
        <input id="email" type="email" formControlName="email" />
      </div>
      <button type="submit">Submit</button>
    </form>

})
export class AppComponent implements OnInit {
  form: FormGroup;

  constructor(private formBuilder: FormBuilder) {}

  ngOnInit() {
    this.form = this.formBuilder.group({
      name: [''],
      email: ['']
    });
  }

  onSubmit(form: FormGroup) {
    console.log(form.value);
  }
}
```

Notice how we inject the formBuilder service in the constructor, and use the group method to create and initialize the form property, which is a FormGroup instance. The group method takes an object that maps the names of the form fields to the initial values or the FormControl instances. In this case, we pass an object with the name and email properties, and assign them empty strings as the initial values. The rest of the code is the same as before.

Form controls and form groups can also be nested within each other, to create more complex forms. For example, let's create a form that collects the user's name, email, and address, where the address is a nested form group that contains the street, city, and zip code fields:

```
import { Component, OnInit } from '@angular/core';
import { FormGroup, FormBuilder } from '@angular/forms';

@Component({
  selector: 'app-root',
  template: `
    <form [formGroup]="form" #form="ngForm"
(ngSubmit)="onSubmit(form)">
      <div>
        <label for="name">Name:</label>
        <input id="name" type="text" formControlName="name" />
      </div>
      <div>
        <label for="email">Email:</label>
        <input id="email" type="email" formControlName="email" />
      </div>
      <div formGroupName="address">
        <div>
          <label for="street">Street:</label>
          <input id="street" type="text" formControlName="street" />
        </div>
        <div>
          <label for="city">City:</label>
          <input id="city" type="text" formControlName="city" />
        </div>
        <div>
          <label for="zip">Zip:</label>
          <input id="zip" type="text" formControlName="zip" />
        </div>
```

```
      </div>
      <button type="submit">Submit</button>
    </form>
      `
})
export class AppComponent implements OnInit {
  form: FormGroup;

  constructor(private formBuilder: FormBuilder) {}

  ngOnInit() {
    this.form = this.formBuilder.group({
      name: [''],
      email: [''],
      address: this.formBuilder.group({
        street: [''],
        city: [''],
        zip: ['']
      })
    });
  }

  onSubmit(form: FormGroup) {
    console.log(form.value);
  }
}
```

Notice how we use the formBuilder.group method to create and initialize a nested form group for the address property, and pass an object with the street, city, and zip properties. We then use the [formGroupName] input property to bind the <div> element to the address property, and the [formControlName] input property to bind the <input> elements to the street, city, and zip properties. The rest of the code is the same as before.

How to use validators and custom validators

Validators are functions that check whether a form field or a form group meets some criteria or rules, and return an error object if not. Validators are used to validate form fields and form groups, and display error messages or disable the submit button if the form is invalid. Validators can be built-in or custom, and can be synchronous or asynchronous.

Built-in validators are provided by Angular, and can be imported from @angular/forms. Built-in validators include required, minLength, maxLength, min, max, pattern, email, etc. Built-in validators can be applied to form controls or form groups, using the validators property of the FormControl or FormGroup constructor, or the formBuilder service. The validators property takes an array of validator functions, which can be composed using the Validators class, which has static methods such as compose, composeAsync, nullValidator, etc. For example, let's modify the previous example to add some built-in validators to the form fields:

```
import { Component, OnInit } from '@angular/core';
import { FormGroup, FormBuilder, Validators } from '@angular/forms';

@Component({
  selector: 'app-root',
  template: `
    <form [formGroup]="form" #form="ngForm"
(ngSubmit)="onSubmit(form)">
      <div>
        <label for="name">Name:</label>
        <input id="name" type="text" formControlName="name" />
        <div *ngIf="form.get('name').invalid &&
form.get('name').touched">
          <span *ngIf="form.get('name').errors.required">Name is
required</span>
          <span *ngIf="form.get('name').errors.minLength">
            Name must be at least 3 characters long
          </span>
        </div>
```

```html
      </div>
      <div>
        <label for="email">Email:</label>
        <input id="email" type="email" formControlName="email" />
        <div *ngIf="form.get('email').invalid &&
form.get('email').touched">
          <span *ngIf="form.get('email').errors.required">Email is
required</span>
          <span *ngIf="form.get('email').errors.email">Email is
invalid</span>
        </div>
      </div>
      <div formGroupName="address">
        <div>
          <label for="street">Street:</label>
          <input id="street" type="text" formControlName="street" />
          <div
            *ngIf="form.get('address.street').invalid &&
form.get('address.street').touched"
          >
            <span *ngIf="form.get('address.street').errors.required"
              >Street is required</span
            >
          </div>
        </div>
        <div>
          <label for="city">City:</label>
          <input id="city" type="text" formControlName="city" />
          <div *ngIf="form.get('address.city').invalid &&
form.get('address.city').touched">
            <span
*ngIf="form.get('address.city').errors.required">City is
required</span>
          </div>
        </div>
        <div>
          <label for="zip">Zip:</label>
          <input id="zip" type="text" formControlName="zip" />
          <div *ngIf="form.get('address.zip').invalid &&
form.get('address.zip').touched">
```

```
            <span *ngIf="form.get('address.zip').errors.required">Zip
is required</span>
            <span *ngIf="form.get('address.zip').errors.pattern"
              >Zip must be a 5-digit number</span
            >
          </div>
        </div>
      </div>
      <button type="submit" [disabled]="form.invalid">Submit</button>
    </form>

})
export class AppComponent implements OnInit {
  form: FormGroup;

  constructor(private formBuilder: FormBuilder) {}

  ngOnInit() {
    this.form = this.formBuilder.group({
      name: ['', [Validators.required, Validators.minLength(3)]],
      email: ['', [Validators.required, Validators.email]],
      address: this.formBuilder.group({
        street: ['', Validators.required],
        city: ['', Validators.required],
        zip: ['', [Validators.required,
Validators.pattern(/^\d{5}$/)]]
      })
    });
  }

  onSubmit(form: FormGroup) {
    console.log(form.value);
  }
}
```

Notice how we import the Validators class from @angular/forms, and use it to apply some built-in validators to the form fields, such as required, minLength, email, pattern, etc. We pass an array of validator functions to the validators property of the formBuilder.group or formBuilder.control methods, which create and initialize the form controls and form groups. We then use the *ngIf directive to display some error messages in the template, based on the invalid and touched properties of the form fields. We also use the errors property of the form fields to access the error object returned by the validators, and display the corresponding error message. We also use the [disabled] input property to disable the submit button if the form is invalid, using the invalid property of the form.

Custom validators are functions that implement your own validation logic, and return an error object if the form field or form group does not meet your criteria or rules. Custom validators can be synchronous or asynchronous, and can be applied to form controls or form groups, using the same validators property as the built-in validators. Custom validators can also be reusable, by creating a function that returns a validator function, and optionally using the @Injectable decorator to make it injectable in any component. For example, let's create a custom validator that checks whether the name field contains the word "admin", and returns an error object if so:

```
import { Injectable } from '@angular/core';
import { AbstractControl, ValidatorFn } from '@angular/forms';

@Injectable({
  providedIn: 'root'
})
export class CustomValidatorsService {
  forbiddenNameValidator(forbiddenName: string): ValidatorFn {
    return (control: AbstractControl): { [key: string]: any } | null
=> {
      const forbidden =
control.value.toLowerCase().includes(forbiddenName.toLowerCase());
      return forbidden ? { forbiddenName: { value: control.value } }
: null;
    };
```

```
    }
  }
```

Notice how we create a function that takes a forbiddenName parameter, and returns a validator function. The validator function takes an AbstractControl parameter, which is a base class for FormControl and FormGroup, and returns an error object or null. The error object has a key that represents the name of the error, and a value that represents the invalid value. The validator function checks whether the control value contains the forbidden name, and returns the error object if so, or null otherwise. We also use the @Injectable decorator to make the function injectable in any component.

To use the custom validator, we need to inject it in the constructor of the component class, and use it in the validators property of the form control or form group.

How to use dynamic forms and form arrays

Dynamic forms are forms that can be created and modified at runtime, based on some data or logic. Dynamic forms are useful when you don't know the number or the type of the form fields in advance, or when you want to give the user the option to add or remove form fields dynamically. Dynamic forms can be created using reactive forms and form arrays.

Form arrays are a subclass of form groups that represent an array of form controls or form groups. Form arrays have properties and methods that allow you to access and manipulate the form data and state, such as controls, at, push, insert, removeAt, etc. Form arrays can be created and initialized using the FormArray class or the formBuilder.array method, which take an array of form controls or form groups as an argument.

To display a form array, you need to use the <div> element with the [formArrayName] input property, and bind it to the name of the form array. You also need to use the *ngFor directive to iterate over the form array controls, and use the [formGroupName] or [formControlName] input property to bind the <div> or the input elements to the form array controls. You can also use the formArray instance to add or remove form controls or form groups dynamically, using the push, insert, or removeAt methods. For example, let's create a dynamic form that collects the user's hobbies, and allows the user to add or remove hobbies dynamically:

```
import { Component, OnInit } from '@angular/core';
import { FormGroup, FormBuilder, FormArray } from '@angular/forms';

@Component({
  selector: 'app-root',
  template: `
    <form [formGroup]="form" #form="ngForm"
(ngSubmit)="onSubmit(form)">
      <div>
        <label for="name">Name:</label>
        <input id="name" type="text" formControlName="name" />
      </div>
      <div formArrayName="hobbies">
        <div *ngFor="let hobby of hobbies.controls; let i = index"
[formGroupName]="i">
          <label for="hobby-{{i}}">Hobby {{i + 1}}:</label>
          <input id="hobby-{{i}}" type="text" formControlName="name"
/>
          <button (click)="removeHobby(i)">Remove</button>
        </div>
      </div>
      <button (click)="addHobby()">Add Hobby</button>
      <button type="submit">Submit</button>
    </form>

})
```

```
export class AppComponent implements OnInit {
  form: FormGroup;

  constructor(private formBuilder: FormBuilder) {}

  ngOnInit() {
    this.form = this.formBuilder.group({
      name: [''],
      hobbies: this.formBuilder.array([])
    });
  }

  get hobbies() {
    return this.form.get('hobbies') as FormArray;
  }

  addHobby() {
    this.hobbies.push(this.formBuilder.group({ name: [''] }));
  }

  removeHobby(index: number) {
    this.hobbies.removeAt(index);
  }

  onSubmit(form: FormGroup) {
    console.log(form.value);
  }
}
```

Notice how we use the formBuilder.array method to create and initialize a form array for the hobbies property, and pass an empty array as the initial value. We then use the [formArrayName] input property to bind the <div> element to the hobbies property, and the *ngFor directive to iterate over the hobbies.controls array, which contains the form groups for each hobby. We also use the [formGroupName] input property to bind the nested <div> element to the index of the form group, and the [formControlName] input property to bind the <input> element to the name property of the form group. We then use the <button> elements with the (click) output property to trigger the addHobby and removeHobby methods, which use the push and removeAt methods of the form array to add or remove form groups dynamically. The rest of the code is the same as before.

This concludes the chapter on forms and validation. In this chapter, we learned about:

- What are forms and how to use them using the FormsModule and the ReactiveFormsModule
- How to use template-driven forms and the ngModel and ngForm directives
- How to use reactive forms and the FormControl, FormGroup, and FormArray classes
- How to use form controls and form groups to create and manipulate form fields
- How to use validators and custom validators to validate form fields and display error messages
- How to use dynamic forms and form arrays to create and manage forms dynamically

We hope you enjoyed this chapter and learned something new. In the next chapter, we will explore the topic of HTTP and observables in Angular.

6 HTTP AND APIS

In this chapter, you will learn how to communicate with web servers and APIs using the HTTP protocol in Angular 17. You will learn how to use the HttpClient service and interceptors, how to make different types of HTTP requests, how to handle errors and retries, and how to use JSON Web Tokens and authentication.

What is HTTP and how to use it

HTTP stands for Hypertext Transfer Protocol. It is a standard protocol that defines how web browsers and web servers communicate over the internet. HTTP works by sending requests and receiving responses. A request consists of a method, a URL, some headers, and an optional body. A response consists of a status code, some headers, and an optional body.

HTTP methods indicate the action that the client wants to perform on the server. The most common methods are GET, POST, PUT, and DELETE. GET requests are used to retrieve data from the server, POST requests are used to send data to the server, PUT requests are used to update data on the server, and DELETE requests are used to delete data from the server.

HTTP URLs identify the resource that the client wants to access on the server. A URL consists of a scheme, a host, a port, a path, and an optional query string. For example, the URL http://example.com:3000/users?name=John has the scheme http, the host example.com, the port 3000, the path /users, and the query string name=John.

HTTP headers provide additional information about the request or the response. Headers are key-value pairs that can specify things like the content type, the content length, the authorization, the cache control, and the cookies. For example, the header Content-Type: application/json indicates that the body of the request or the response is in JSON format.

HTTP bodies contain the actual data that the client or the server wants to send or receive. Bodies are optional and can be in different formats, such as plain text, HTML, XML, JSON, or binary. For example, the body {"name":"John","age":25} is a JSON object that represents a user.

To use HTTP in Angular 17, you need to import the HttpClientModule from @angular/common/http and inject the HttpClient service in your components or services. The HttpClient service provides methods to make HTTP requests and returns observables that emit the responses. For example, to make a GET request to http://example.com/users, you can write:

```
import { Component, OnInit } from '@angular/core';
import { HttpClient } from '@angular/common/http';

@Component({
  selector: 'app-users',
  templateUrl: './users.component.html',
  styleUrls: ['./users.component.css']
})
export class UsersComponent implements OnInit {
```

```
  users: any[] = [];

  constructor(private http: HttpClient) { }

  ngOnInit(): void {
    this.http.get('http://example.com/users')
      .subscribe(response => {
        this.users = response;
      });
  }
}
```

How to use the HttpClient service and interceptors

The HttpClient service provides several methods to make different types of HTTP requests, such as get(), post(), put(), delete(), patch(), and head(). Each method takes a URL as the first argument, and optionally a body as the second argument, and an options object as the third argument. The options object can specify things like the headers, the parameters, the responseType, and the observe mode. For example, to make a POST request to http://example.com/users with a JSON body and a custom header, you can write:

```
import { Component, OnInit } from '@angular/core';
import { HttpClient } from '@angular/common/http';

@Component({
  selector: 'app-add-user',
  templateUrl: './add-user.component.html',
  styleUrls: ['./add-user.component.css']
})
export class AddUserComponent implements OnInit {

  user: any = {};

  constructor(private http: HttpClient) { }
```

```
  ngOnInit(): void {
  }

  addUser(): void {
    this.http.post('http://example.com/users', this.user, {
      headers: {
        'X-Custom-Header': 'Angular 17'
      }
    })
      .subscribe(response => {
        console.log(response);
      });
  }

}
```

The HttpClient service returns observables that emit the responses from the server. You can subscribe to these observables and handle the responses in your components or services. You can also use RxJS operators to transform, filter, or combine the observables. For example, to map the response to a custom format, you can write:

```
import { Component, OnInit } from '@angular/core';
import { HttpClient } from '@angular/common/http';
import { map } from 'rxjs/operators';

@Component({
  selector: 'app-users',
  templateUrl: './users.component.html',
  styleUrls: ['./users.component.css']
})
export class UsersComponent implements OnInit {

  users: any[] = [];

  constructor(private http: HttpClient) { }
```

```
ngOnInit(): void {
  this.http.get('http://example.com/users')
    .pipe(
      map(response => response.map(user => ({
        id: user.id,
        name: user.name.toUpperCase(),
        age: user.age + 1
      }))) 
    )
    .subscribe(response => {
      this.users = response;
    });
  }


}
```

Interceptors are classes that implement the HttpInterceptor interface and provide a intercept() method that can intercept and modify the HTTP requests and responses. You can use interceptors to add common headers, log requests and responses, handle errors, or implement caching. To use interceptors, you need to provide them in the providers array of your AppModule with the HTTP_INTERCEPTORS token. For example, to create and use a logging interceptor, you can write:

```
import { Injectable } from '@angular/core';
import { HttpInterceptor, HttpRequest, HttpHandler, HttpEvent } from '@angular/common/http';
import { Observable } from 'rxjs';
import { tap } from 'rxjs/operators';

@Injectable()
export class LoggingInterceptor implements HttpInterceptor {

  intercept(req: HttpRequest<any>, next: HttpHandler):
Observable<HttpEvent<any>> {
    console.log('Request:', req);
    return next.handle(req)
```

```
      .pipe(
        tap(event => {
          console.log('Response:', event);
        })
      );
  }

}


// In app.module.ts

import { NgModule } from '@angular/core';
import { BrowserModule } from '@angular/platform-browser';
import { HttpClientModule, HTTP_INTERCEPTORS } from
'@angular/common/http';
import { AppComponent } from './app.component';
import { LoggingInterceptor } from './logging.interceptor';


@NgModule({
  declarations: [
    AppComponent
  ],
  imports: [
    BrowserModule,
    HttpClientModule
  ],
  providers: [
    {
      provide: HTTP_INTERCEPTORS,
      useClass: LoggingInterceptor,
      multi: true
    }
  ],
  bootstrap: [AppComponent]
})
export class AppModule { }
```

How to make GET, POST, PUT, and DELETE requests

As mentioned before, the HttpClient service provides methods to make different types of HTTP requests, such as get(), post(), put(), and delete(). Each method takes a URL as the first argument, and optionally a body as the second argument, and an options object as the third argument. The options object can specify things like the headers, the parameters, the responseType, and the observe mode.

GET requests are used to retrieve data from the server. You can use the get() method to make a GET request. For example, to get a list of users from http://example.com/users, you can write:

```
this.http.get('http://example.com/users')
  .subscribe(response => {
    console.log(response);
  });
```

POST requests are used to send data to the server. You can use the post() method to make a POST request. You need to provide a body as the second argument. For example, to create a new user on http://example.com/users, you can write:

```
this.http.post('http://example.com/users', {
  name: 'Alice',
  age: 22
})
  .subscribe(response => {
    console.log(response);
  });
```

PUT requests are used to update data on the server. You can use the put() method to make a PUT request. You need to provide a body as the second argument. For example, to update the name of a user with id 1 on http://example.com/users/1, you can write:

```
this.http.put('http://example.com/users/1', {
  name: 'Bob'
})
  .subscribe(response => {
    console.log(response);
  });
```

DELETE requests are used to delete data from the server. You can use the delete() method to make a DELETE request. For example, to delete a user with id 1 from http://example.com/users/1, you can write:

```
this.http.delete('http://example.com/users/1')
  .subscribe(response => {
    console.log(response);
  });
```

How to handle errors and retries

Sometimes, the HTTP requests may fail due to various reasons, such as network issues, server errors, or invalid inputs. You need to handle these errors gracefully and provide appropriate feedback to the user. You can also retry the requests if the errors are transient or recoverable.

To handle errors and retries, you can use the catchError and retry operators from RxJS. The catchError operator lets you catch and handle the errors from the observable. You can return a new observable or throw an error. The retry operator lets you retry the observable a specified number of times. For example, to catch and log the errors and retry the request up to 3 times, you can write:

```
import { Component, OnInit } from '@angular/core';
import { HttpClient } from '@angular/common/http';
```

```
import { catchError, retry } from 'rxjs/operators';
import { throwError } from 'rxjs';

@Component({
  selector: 'app-users',
  templateUrl: './users.component.html',
  styleUrls: ['./users.component.css']
})
export class UsersComponent implements OnInit {

  users: any[] = [];

  constructor(private http: HttpClient) { }

  ngOnInit(): void {
    this.http.get('http://example.com/users')
      .pipe(
        retry(3),
        catchError(error => {
          console.error(error);
          return throwError(error);
        })
      )
      .subscribe(response => {
        this.users = response;
      });
  }

}
```

How to use JSON Web Tokens and authentication

JSON Web Tokens (JWT) are a standard way of representing claims or information between two parties. A JWT consists of three parts: a header, a payload, and a signature. The header contains the algorithm and the type of the token. The payload contains the claims or information, such as the user id, the expiration time, or the roles. The signature is computed by applying the algorithm to the header and the payload, and using a secret key. The three parts are encoded in base64 and separated by dots. For example, a JWT may look like this:

```
eyJhbGciOiJIUzI1NiIsInR5cCI6IkpXVCJ9.eyJ1c2VySWQiOjEsImV4cCI6MTY0MTYw
MzE5NSwicm9sZXMiOlsiYWRtaW4iLCJ1c2VyIl19.1t8Z1L8b7xQyZG9nZ6f0Y4a0g3p5
q7xq0XZ8f0g0FZk
```

To use JWT and authentication in Angular 17, you need to implement a service that can generate, store, and verify the tokens. You also need to implement an interceptor that can attach the tokens to the HTTP requests. For example, to create and use a JWT service and an auth interceptor, you can write:

```
import { Injectable } from '@angular/core';
import { JwtHelperService } from '@auth0/angular-jwt';

@Injectable()
export class JwtService {

  private jwtHelper: JwtHelperService;

  constructor() {
    this.jwtHelper = new JwtHelperService();
  }

  // Generate a token for testing purposes
  generateToken(): string {
    const header = {
      alg: 'HS256',
      typ: 'JWT'
    };
    const payload = {
      userId: 1,
      exp: Math.floor(Date.now() / 1000) + 60 * 60, // 1 hour
      roles: ['admin', 'user']
    };
    const secret = 'secret';
    return this.jwtHelper.encodeToken(payload, header, secret);
```

```
}

// Store the token in the local storage
storeToken(token: string): void {
  localStorage.setItem('token', token);
}

// Get the token from the local storage
getToken(): string | null {
  return localStorage.getItem('token');
}

// Remove the token from the local storage
removeToken(): void {
  localStorage.removeItem('token');
}

// Check if the token is valid and not expired
isValidToken(): boolean {
  const token = this.getToken();
  if (token) {
    return !this.jwtHelper.isTokenExpired(token);
  }
  return false;
}

// Get the user id from the token
getUserId(): number | null {
  const token = this.getToken();
  if (token) {
    const decoded = this.jwtHelper.decodeToken(token);
    return decoded.userId;
  }
  return null;
}

// Get the roles from the token
getRoles(): string[] | null {
  const token = this.getToken();
```

```
    if (token) {
      const decoded = this.jwtHelper.decodeToken(token);
      return decoded.roles;
    }
    return null;
  }

}


// In auth.interceptor.ts

import { Injectable } from '@angular/core';
import { HttpInterceptor, HttpRequest, HttpHandler, HttpEvent } from
'@angular/common/http';
import { Observable } from 'rxjs';
import { JwtService } from './jwt.service';

@Injectable()
export class AuthInterceptor implements HttpInterceptor {

  constructor(private jwtService: JwtService) { }

  intercept(req: HttpRequest<any>, next: HttpHandler):
Observable<HttpEvent<any>> {
    const token = this.jwtService.getToken();
    if (token) {
      // Clone the request and add the Authorization header
      const authReq = req.clone({
        headers: req.headers.set('Authorization', 'Bearer ' + token)
      });
      return next.handle(authReq);
    }
    return next.handle(req);
  }

}


// In app.module.ts
```

```
import { NgModule } from '@angular/core';
import { BrowserModule } from '@angular/platform-browser';
import { HttpClientModule, HTTP_INTERCEPTORS } from
'@angular/common/http';
import { AppComponent } from './app.component';
import { JwtService } from './jwt.service';
import { AuthInterceptor } from './auth.interceptor';

@NgModule({
  declarations: [
    AppComponent
  ],
  imports: [
    BrowserModule,
    HttpClientModule
  ],
  providers: [
    JwtService,
    {
      provide: HTTP_INTERCEPTORS,
      useClass: AuthInterceptor,
      multi: true
    }
  ],
  bootstrap: [AppComponent]
})
export class AppModule { }
```

This is the end of the chapter. You have learned how to use HTTP and APIs in Angular 17, how to use the HttpClient service and interceptors, how to make different types of HTTP requests, how to handle errors and retries, and how to use JSON Web Tokens and authentication. You can now use these skills to build web applications that can communicate with web servers and APIs securely and efficiently.

7 TESTING AND DEBUGGING

In this chapter, you will learn how to test and debug your Angular 17 applications using various tools and techniques. You will learn how to use Jasmine and Karma for unit testing, how to use Protractor and Cypress for end-to-end testing, how to use the Angular CLI and Chrome DevTools for debugging, and how to use the Angular Language Service and VS Code for code completion.

What is testing and why is it important

Testing is the process of verifying that your application works as expected and meets the requirements. Testing helps you find and fix errors, improve the quality and reliability of your code, and prevent future bugs and regressions.

There are different types of testing, such as:

- Unit testing: testing small, isolated pieces of code, such as functions, components, or services

- Integration testing: testing how different parts of your application work together, such as modules, directives, or pipes

- End-to-end testing: testing the functionality of your application from a user perspective, such as navigating, clicking, or filling forms
- Performance testing: testing how fast and responsive your application is, such as loading time, memory usage, or network requests

Testing is important because it:
- Saves time and money: testing helps you avoid costly and time-consuming errors in production, and reduces the need for manual testing and debugging
- Increases confidence and trust: testing ensures that your application meets the expectations and needs of your users and stakeholders, and that it is secure and stable
- Enhances collaboration and communication: testing helps you document and share your code behavior and functionality, and facilitates feedback and review from your team and clients

How to use Jasmine and Karma for unit testing

Jasmine and Karma are the default tools for unit testing in Angular 17. Jasmine is a testing framework that provides syntax and utilities for writing and running tests. Karma is a test runner that launches browsers and executes tests.

The Angular CLI sets up everything you need to use Jasmine and Karma for unit testing. The project you create with the CLI is ready to test. Just run the ng test command:

```
ng test
```

The ng test command builds the application in watch mode, and launches the Karma test runner. The console output looks like this:

```
02 11 2022 09:08:28.605:INFO [karma-server]: Karma v6.4.1 server
started at http://localhost:9876/
02 11 2022 09:08:28.607:INFO [launcher]: Launching browsers Chrome
with concurrency unlimited
02 11 2022 09:08:28.620:INFO [launcher]: Starting browser Chrome
02 11 2022 09:08:31.312:INFO [Chrome]: Connected on socket -
LaEYvD2R7MdcS0-AAAB with id 31534482
Chrome: Executed 3 of 3 SUCCESS (0.193 secs / 0.172 secs)
TOTAL: 3 SUCCESS
```

The last line of the log shows that Karma ran three tests that all passed. The test output is displayed in the browser using Karma Jasmine HTML Reporter. Click on a test row to re-run just that test or click on a description to re-run the tests in the selected test group (test suite).

Meanwhile, the ng test command is watching for changes. To see this in action, make a small change to app.component.ts and save. The tests run again, the browser refreshes, and the new test results appear.

Test file name and location

Inside the src/app folder the Angular CLI generated a test file for the AppComponent named app.component.spec.ts. The test file extension must be .spec.ts so that tooling can identify it as a file with tests (also known as a spec file). The app.component.ts and app.component.spec.ts files are siblings in the same folder. The root file names (app.component) are the same for both files.

You should follow the same naming and location conventions for your own test files. For example, if you have a component named hello.component.ts in the src/app/hello folder, you should create a test file named hello.component.spec.ts in the same folder.

Test structure and syntax

A test file typically contains one or more test suites, and each test suite contains one or more test cases. A test suite is a collection of tests that are related to a specific part of your application, such as a component, a service, or a pipe. A test case is a single unit of testing that verifies a specific behavior or functionality of your application.

Jasmine provides a syntax and a set of functions to write and organize your tests. The most common functions are:

- describe: defines a test suite. It takes two arguments: a string that describes the test suite, and a function that contains the test cases
- it: defines a test case. It takes two arguments: a string that describes the test case, and a function that contains the test logic and expectations
- expect: defines an expectation. It takes one argument: the actual value to be tested. It returns an object that has various methods to assert the expected value or condition, such as toBe, toEqual, toBeTruthy, toContain, etc.

For example, this is how a test suite for the AppComponent looks like:

```
import { TestBed } from '@angular/core/testing';
import { AppComponent } from './app.component';

describe('AppComponent', () => {
  beforeEach(async () => {
    await TestBed.configureTestingModule({
      declarations: [
        AppComponent
      ],
    }).compileComponents();
  });

  it('should create the app', () => {
    const fixture = TestBed.createComponent(AppComponent);
    const app = fixture.componentInstance;
    expect(app).toBeTruthy();
```

```
  });

  it(`should have as title 'angular-testing'`, () => {
    const fixture = TestBed.createComponent(AppComponent);
    const app = fixture.componentInstance;
    expect(app.title).toEqual('angular-testing');
  });

  it('should render title', () => {
    const fixture = TestBed.createComponent(AppComponent);
    fixture.detectChanges();
    const compiled = fixture.nativeElement;
    expect(compiled.querySelector('.content
span').textContent).toContain('angular-testing app is running!');
  });
});
```

The first describe function defines the test suite for the AppComponent. The second argument is a function that contains the test cases for the component.

The beforeEach function is a special function that runs before each test case. It is used to set up the testing environment, such as creating and configuring the testing module, injecting dependencies, or initializing variables.

The it functions define the test cases for the component. Each test case has a descriptive string and a function that contains the test logic and expectations. The test logic usually involves creating a component instance, accessing its properties or methods, triggering events or changes, and checking the results. The expectations use the expect function and its methods to assert the actual and expected values or conditions.

Testing utilities

To write and run tests for Angular components, you need to use some testing utilities provided by Angular. The most important ones are:

- TestBed: a testing module that allows you to create and configure a testing version of your application module, with mock dependencies, providers, and declarations
- ComponentFixture: a testing fixture that allows you to create and access a component instance, its template, its change detector, and its debug element
- DebugElement: a wrapper around a native DOM element that provides access to the component instance, the injector, the listeners, and the child elements

These utilities are imported from @angular/core/testing and are used in the test cases to interact with the component under test. For example, to create and test a component instance, you can write:

```
import { TestBed, ComponentFixture } from '@angular/core/testing';
import { AppComponent } from './app.component';

describe('AppComponent', () => {
  let fixture: ComponentFixture<AppComponent>;
  let component: AppComponent;

  beforeEach(async () => {
    await TestBed.configureTestingModule({
      declarations: [
        AppComponent
      ],
    }).compileComponents();
    fixture = TestBed.createComponent(AppComponent);
    component = fixture.componentInstance;
  });

  it('should create the app', () => {
    expect(component).toBeTruthy();
  });

  // more test cases ...
});
```

The TestBed.configureTestingModule method creates and configures a testing module with the same declarations as the AppModule. The compileComponents method compiles the components asynchronously.

The TestBed.createComponent method creates a component fixture for the AppComponent. The component fixture provides access to the component instance through the componentInstance property.

The expect function checks that the component instance is truthy, meaning that it is not null, undefined, false, 0, or ".

How to use Protractor and Cypress for end-to-end testing

End-to-end testing is the process of testing the functionality of your application from a user perspective, such as navigating, clicking, or filling forms. End-to-end testing involves launching a browser, loading your application, and interacting with it as a real user would.

Protractor and Cypress are two popular tools for end-to-end testing in Angular 17. Protractor is the default tool for end-to-end testing in Angular 17, but Cypress is a newer and more modern alternative that offers some advantages over Protractor, such as faster and more reliable execution, better debugging experience, and native support for TypeScript.

The ng e2e command launches the Protractor or Cypress test runner and runs the end-to-end tests. The console output looks like this:

```
ng e2e

Compiling @angular/core : es2015 as esm2015
```

```
Compiling @angular/common : es2015 as esm2015
Compiling @angular/platform-browser : es2015 as esm2015
Compiling @angular/platform-browser-dynamic : es2015 as esm2015
Compiling @angular/router : es2015 as esm2015
chunk {main} main.js, main.js.map (main) 47.9 kB [initial] [rendered]
chunk {polyfills} polyfills.js, polyfills.js.map (polyfills) 141 kB
[initial] [rendered]
chunk {runtime} runtime.js, runtime.js.map (runtime) 6.15 kB [entry]
[rendered]
chunk {styles} styles.js, styles.js.map (styles) 16.3 kB [initial]
[rendered]
chunk {vendor} vendor.js, vendor.js.map (vendor) 2.66 MB [initial]
[rendered]
Date: 2022-11-02T09:12:34.123Z - Hash: 1234abcd - Time: 12345ms
** Angular Live Development Server is listening on localhost:4200,
open your browser on http://localhost:4200/ **
: Compiled successfully.


[09:12:34] I/launcher - Running 1 instances of WebDriver
[09:12:34] I/direct - Using ChromeDriver directly...
Jasmine started

  angular-testing App
    √ should display welcome message
    √ should display title
    √ should increment counter

Executed 3 of 3 specs SUCCESS in 3 secs.
[09:12:38] I/launcher - 0 instance(s) of WebDriver still running
[09:12:38] I/launcher - chrome #01 passed
```

The last line of the log shows that Protractor or Cypress ran three tests that all passed. The test output is displayed in the browser using Jasmine HTML Reporter. You can also see the screenshots and videos of the tests in the e2e folder.

Test file name and location

Inside the e2e folder the Angular CLI generated a test file for the AppComponent named app.e2e-spec.ts. The test file extension must be .e2e-spec.ts so that tooling can identify it as a file with end-to-end tests. The app.e2e-spec.ts file is in the same folder as the app.po.ts file, which is a page object file that provides helper methods to access and interact with the elements of the AppComponent.

You should follow the same naming and location conventions for your own test files. For example, if you have a component named hello.component.ts in the src/app/hello folder, you should create a test file named hello.e2e-spec.ts and a page object file named hello.po.ts in the e2e/src/app/hello folder.

Test structure and syntax

A test file typically contains one or more test suites, and each test suite contains one or more test cases. A test suite is a collection of tests that are related to a specific part of your application, such as a component, a page, or a feature. A test case is a single unit of testing that verifies a specific behavior or functionality of your application.

Protractor and Cypress use Jasmine as the testing framework, so the syntax and the functions are the same as for unit testing. The most common functions are:

- describe: defines a test suite. It takes two arguments: a string that describes the test suite, and a function that contains the test cases
- it: defines a test case. It takes two arguments: a string that describes the test case, and a function that contains the test logic and expectations
- expect: defines an expectation. It takes one argument: the actual value to be tested. It returns an object that has various methods to assert the expected value or condition, such as toBe, toEqual, toBeTruthy, toContain, etc.

For example, this is how a test suite for the AppComponent looks like:

```
import { AppPage } from './app.po';

describe('angular-testing App', () => {
  let page: AppPage;

  beforeEach(() => {
    page = new AppPage();
  });

  it('should display welcome message', () => {
    page.navigateTo();
    expect(page.getTitleText()).toEqual('Welcome to angular-
testing!');
  });

  it('should display title', () => {
    page.navigateTo();
    expect(page.getParagraphText()).toEqual('angular-testing app is
running!');
  });

  it('should increment counter', () => {
    page.navigateTo();
    expect(page.getCounterText()).toEqual('0');
    page.clickIncrementButton();
    expect(page.getCounterText()).toEqual('1');
  });
});
```

The first describe function defines the test suite for the AppComponent. The second argument is a function that contains the test cases for the component.

The beforeEach function is a special function that runs before each test case. It is used to set up the testing environment, such as creating and initializing the page object.

The it functions define the test cases for the component. Each test case has a descriptive string and a function that contains the test logic and expectations. The test logic usually involves navigating to the component page, accessing and interacting with its elements, and checking the results. The expectations use the expect function and its methods to assert the actual and expected values or conditions.

Testing utilities

To write and run tests for Angular components, you need to use some testing utilities provided by Protractor or Cypress. The most important ones are:

- browser: a global object that represents the browser instance that Protractor or Cypress controls. It provides methods to navigate, wait, execute scripts, manage cookies, and access the current URL, title, and window

- element: a global function that returns an ElementFinder object that represents a DOM element on the page. It takes a locator argument that specifies how to find the element, such as by id, class, tag, css, or xpath

- by: a global object that provides various locator strategies to find elements on the page, such as by.id, by.className, by.tagName, by.css, or by.xpath

- ElementFinder: an object that represents a DOM element on the page. It provides methods to get and set its properties, such as text, value, attribute, or class. It also provides methods to interact with it, such as click, sendKeys, clear, or submit

- ElementArrayFinder: an object that represents a collection of DOM elements on the page. It provides methods to filter, map, reduce, count, or get the elements. It also provides methods to access the first or the last element, or the element at a specific index

These utilities are imported from protractor or cypress and are used in the test cases to interact with the component under test. For example, to access and test a component element, you can write:

```
import { browser, element, by } from 'protractor';

describe('AppComponent', () => {

  it('should display title', () => {
    browser.get('http://localhost:4200/');
    const title = element(by.css('.content span'));
    expect(title.getText()).toEqual('angular-testing app is
running!');
  });

  // more test cases ...
});
```

The browser.get method navigates to the component page by its URL.

The element function returns an ElementFinder object that represents the title element on the page. It takes a by.css locator that specifies how to find the element by its CSS selector.

The expect function checks that the text of the title element is equal to the expected value. The getText method returns the text content of the element.

How to use the Angular CLI and Chrome DevTools for debugging

Debugging is the process of finding and fixing errors in your application. Debugging helps you understand and improve the logic and behavior of your code, and prevent future bugs and regressions.

The Angular CLI and Chrome DevTools are the default tools for debugging in Angular 17. The Angular CLI is a command-line interface that provides various commands and options to build, serve, test, and debug your application. Chrome DevTools is a set of web developer tools that are built into the Chrome browser. Chrome DevTools provides various features and panels to inspect, modify, and monitor your application, such as Elements, Console, Sources, Network, Performance, Memory, and Application.

The Angular CLI sets up everything you need to use Chrome DevTools for debugging. The project you create with the CLI is ready to debug. Just run the ng serve command:

```
ng serve
```

The ng serve command builds the application in watch mode, and serves it on http://localhost:4200/. The console output looks like this:

```
** Angular Live Development Server is listening on localhost:4200,
open your browser on http://localhost:4200/ **
: Compiled successfully.

Date: 2022-11-02T09:18:34.123Z - Hash: 1234abcd - Time: 12345ms
chunk {main} main.js, main.js.map (main) 47.9 kB [initial] [rendered]
chunk {polyfills} polyfills.js, polyfills.js.map (polyfills) 141 kB
[initial] [rendered]
chunk {runtime} runtime.js, runtime.js.map (runtime) 6.15 kB [entry]
[rendered]
chunk {styles} styles.js, styles.js.map (styles) 16.3 kB [initial]
[rendered]
chunk {vendor} vendor.js, vendor.js.map (vendor) 2.66 MB [initial]
[rendered]
```

The ng serve command also enables the source map support, which allows you to debug your TypeScript code in the browser using Chrome DevTools.

To open Chrome DevTools, you can press Ctrl+Shift+I on Windows or Cmd+Option+I on Mac, or right-click on the page and select Inspect. Chrome DevTools opens in a new window or a panel at the bottom of the browser.

Chrome DevTools provides various features and panels to inspect, modify, and monitor your application, such as:

- Elements: shows the HTML structure and the CSS styles of the page. You can select, edit, or delete elements, and see how they affect the layout and appearance of the page

- Console: shows the log messages, errors, and warnings from the browser and your code. You can also execute JavaScript commands and expressions in the console

- Sources: shows the source files of your application, including the TypeScript files. You can set breakpoints, step through the code, watch variables, and evaluate expressions

- Network: shows the network requests and responses of your application, including the headers, the body, the status, and the timing. You can filter, sort, or search the requests, and see how they affect the performance and functionality of the page

- Performance: shows the performance metrics and the timeline of your application, such as the CPU usage, the memory usage, the frames per second, and the events. You can record, replay, or analyze the performance of your page, and identify the bottlenecks and the optimizations

- Memory: shows the memory usage and the heap snapshots of your application. You can take, compare, or export the snapshots, and see how the memory is allocated and released by your code

- Application: shows the application data and the resources of your application, such as the cookies, the local storage, the session storage, the cache, the service workers, and the manifests. You can add, edit, or delete the data and the resources, and see how they affect the state and the behavior of the page

You can use these features and panels to debug your application in various ways, such as:

- Inspecting and modifying the elements and the styles of the page
- Logging and executing commands and expressions in the console
- Setting breakpoints and stepping through the code in the sources
- Monitoring and analyzing the network requests and responses
- Recording and replaying the performance and the timeline of the page
- Taking and comparing the memory and the heap snapshots
- Adding and deleting the application data and the resources

For example, to debug a component element, you can:

- Select the element in the Elements panel, and see its HTML and CSS properties
- Right-click on the element and select Store as global variable, and access it in the Console panel as temp1
- Right-click on the element and select Break on > subtree modifications, and set a breakpoint in the Sources panel when the element changes
- Right-click on the element and select Copy > Copy selector, and use it in the Network panel to filter the requests related to the element
- Right-click on the element and select Capture node screenshot, and save it as an image file

This is the end of the section. You have learned how to use the Angular CLI and Chrome DevTools for debugging. You can now use these tools to find and fix errors in your application, and improve the logic and behavior of your code.

8 DEPLOYMENT AND OPTIMIZATION

In this chapter, you will learn how to deploy and optimize your Angular 17 applications using various tools and techniques. You will learn how to use the Angular CLI and esbuild for building and bundling, how to use the Angular CLI and ng deploy for deploying, how to use lazy loading and deferrable loading for performance, and how to use service workers and PWA for offline support.

What is deployment and how to do it

Deployment is the process of making your application available to the users on the internet. Deployment involves building, bundling, and uploading your application to a remote server, and configuring the server to serve your application.

There are different options for deployment, such as:

- Hosting services: services that provide web hosting and domain name registration, such as Firebase, Netlify, or GitHub Pages
- Cloud platforms: platforms that provide cloud computing and storage, such as AWS, Azure, or Google Cloud
- Custom servers: servers that you set up and manage yourself, such as Apache, Nginx,

or Node.js

To deploy your application, you need to follow these general steps:

- Build and bundle your application using the Angular CLI and esbuild
- Upload your application to the server using the Angular CLI and ng deploy
- Configure the server to serve your application using the Angular CLI and ng deploy

How to use the Angular CLI and esbuild for building and bundling

The Angular CLI and esbuild are the default tools for building and bundling in Angular 17. The Angular CLI is a command-line interface that provides various commands and options to build, serve, test, and debug your application. Esbuild is a fast and modern bundler that transforms and optimizes your code for production.

The Angular CLI sets up everything you need to use esbuild for building and bundling. The project you create with the CLI is ready to build. Just run the ng build command:

```
ng build
```

The ng build command builds the application for production, and outputs the build artifacts to the dist/project-name/ folder. The console output looks like this:

```
** Angular Live Development Server is listening on localhost:4200,
open your browser on http://localhost:4200/ **
: Compiled successfully.

Date: 2022-11-02T09:24:34.123Z - Hash: 1234abcd - Time: 12345ms
chunk {main} main.js, main.js.map (main) 47.9 kB [initial] [rendered]
chunk {polyfills} polyfills.js, polyfills.js.map (polyfills) 141 kB
[initial] [rendered]
chunk {runtime} runtime.js, runtime.js.map (runtime) 6.15 kB [entry]
[rendered]
chunk {styles} styles.js, styles.js.map (styles) 16.3 kB [initial]
[rendered]
```

```
chunk {vendor} vendor.js, vendor.js.map (vendor) 2.66 MB [initial]
[rendered]
```

The ng build command uses esbuild under the hood to transform and optimize your code for production. Esbuild performs various tasks, such as:

- Transpiling TypeScript to JavaScript
- Minifying and mangling the code
- Tree-shaking and dead code elimination
- Bundling and splitting the code
- Generating source maps and hashes

You can customize the build process by using various options and flags with the ng build command, such as:

- --configuration: specifies the build configuration to use, such as production, development, or custom
- --output-path: specifies the output folder for the build artifacts, such as dist, build, or public
- --watch: enables the watch mode, which rebuilds the application when the source files change
- --aot: enables the ahead-of-time compilation, which compiles the Angular components and templates to JavaScript during the build time, instead of the run time
- --build-optimizer: enables the build optimizer, which applies advanced optimizations to the code, such as removing Angular decorators, pure annotations, and side effects
- --source-map: enables the source map generation, which maps the minified code to the original source code, for easier debugging
- --extract-css: enables the extraction of the CSS styles from the JavaScript bundles, for faster loading and caching
- --named-chunks: enables the named chunks generation, which assigns meaningful

names to the chunks, for easier identification

- --vendor-chunk: enables the vendor chunk generation, which separates the vendor code (such as Angular, RxJS, or Bootstrap) from the application code, for better caching and updating

- --common-chunk: enables the common chunk generation, which separates the common code (such as lazy loaded modules) from the main code, for better performance and loading

For example, to build the application for production, with source maps, named chunks, and vendor chunk, you can write:

```
ng build --configuration production --source-map --named-chunks --
vendor-chunk
```

How to use the Angular CLI and ng deploy for deploying

The Angular CLI and ng deploy are the default tools for deploying in Angular 17. The Angular CLI is a command-line interface that provides various commands and options to build, serve, test, and debug your application. Ng deploy is a command that deploys your application to a hosting service or a cloud platform of your choice.

The Angular CLI sets up everything you need to use ng deploy for deploying. The project you create with the CLI is ready to deploy. Just run the ng deploy command:

```
ng deploy
```

The ng deploy command builds the application for production, and uploads the build artifacts to the server. The console output looks like this:

```
** Angular Live Development Server is listening on localhost:4200,
open your browser on http://localhost:4200/ **
: Compiled successfully.

Date: 2022-11-02T09:24:34.123Z - Hash: 1234abcd - Time: 12345ms
chunk {main} main.js, main.js.map (main) 47.9 kB [initial] [rendered]
chunk {polyfills} polyfills.js, polyfills.js.map (polyfills) 141 kB
[initial] [rendered]
chunk {runtime} runtime.js, runtime.js.map (runtime) 6.15 kB [entry]
[rendered]
chunk {styles} styles.js, styles.js.map (styles) 16.3 kB [initial]
[rendered]
chunk {vendor} vendor.js, vendor.js.map (vendor) 2.66 MB [initial]
[rendered]


Deploying "angular-testing"...


✓ Successfully deployed "angular-testing" to Firebase Hosting.

Project Console: https://console.firebase.google.com/project/angular-
testing/overview
Hosting URL: https://angular-testing.web.app
```

The ng deploy command uses the @angular/fire package under the hood to deploy your application to Firebase Hosting. Firebase Hosting is a hosting service that provides fast and secure web hosting for your static and dynamic content.

You can customize the deploy process by using various options and flags with the ng deploy command, such as:

- --configuration: specifies the build configuration to use, such as production, development, or custom

- --output-path: specifies the output folder for the build artifacts, such as dist, build, or public

- --base-href: specifies the base URL for the application, such as /, /app/, or https://example.com/

- --no-build: skips the build step and deploys the existing build artifacts
- --preview: shows a preview of the deploy, but does not actually deploy
- --dry-run: shows a dry run of the deploy, but does not actually deploy

For example, to deploy the application for production, with a custom base URL, and a dry run, you can write:

```
ng deploy --configuration production --base-href /app/ --dry-run
```

You can also use other hosting services or cloud platforms for deploying your application, such as Netlify, GitHub Pages, AWS, Azure, or Google Cloud. To do that, you need to install and use the corresponding packages and commands, such as @netlify-builder/deploy, angular-cli-ghpages, @angular/cli-aws-s3-deploy, @azure/ng-deploy, or @google-cloud/ng-deploy. You can find more information and documentation on the official Angular website: https://angular.io/guide/deployment#automatic-deployment-with-the-cli.

This is the end of the section. You have learned how to use the Angular CLI and ng deploy for deploying. You can now use these tools to make your application available to the users on the internet.

9 CONCLUSIONS

In this book, you have learned how to use Angular 17 to create modern and powerful web applications. You have learned how to use the Angular CLI, the Angular Language Service, and VS Code to set up and develop your projects. You have learned how to use components, directives, pipes, services, modules, and routing to structure and organize your application. You have learned how to use forms, validation, observables, and HTTP to handle user input and data. You have learned how to use Jasmine, Karma, Protractor, and Cypress to test and debug your application. You have learned how to use the Angular CLI, esbuild, and ng deploy to build and deploy your application. You have learned how to use lazy loading, deferrable loading, service workers, and PWA to optimize and enhance your application.

You have also learned some of the new and exciting features of Angular 17, such as:
- Deferrable views, which allow you to defer the rendering of parts of your application until certain conditions are met, such as user interaction, data availability, or route change
- Built-in control flow, which allows you to use a new block template syntax to write loops, conditionals, and expressions in a declarative and efficient way
- Fresh new look, which reflects the future-looking features and identity of Angular

- Interactive learning journey, which allows you to learn Angular and the Angular CLI at your own pace, directly in the browser

You have come a long way from the beginning of this book, and you should be proud of yourself. You have acquired the skills and knowledge to create amazing web applications with Angular 17. But this is not the end of your learning journey. There is always more to learn and explore with Angular. Here are some suggestions on what you can do next:

How to keep up with Angular updates and news

Angular is a constantly evolving framework that releases new versions every six months, with minor updates every month. To keep up with the latest Angular updates and news, you can:

- Follow the official Angular blog, where the Angular team and the community share announcements, insights, and tips on Angular development
- Follow the official Angular Twitter account, where the Angular team and the community post updates, events, and resources on Angular
- Subscribe to the official Angular newsletter, where the Angular team and the community curate the best Angular content every week
- Watch the official Angular YouTube channel, where the Angular team and the community upload videos, tutorials, and talks on Angular
- Listen to the official Angular podcast, where the Angular team and the community discuss Angular topics, trends, and stories

How to join the Angular community and contribute

Angular has a large and active community of developers, enthusiasts, and experts who are passionate about Angular and web development. To join the Angular community and contribute, you can:

- Join the official Angular Discord server, where you can chat, ask questions, and share your experiences with other Angular developers
- Join the official Angular Gitter channel, where you can chat, ask questions, and share your experiences with other Angular developers
- Join the official Angular Reddit community, where you can post, comment, and vote on Angular topics, questions, and resources
- Join the official Angular Stack Overflow community, where you can ask and answer Angular questions, and earn reputation and badges
- Join the official Angular GitHub repository, where you can report issues, submit pull requests, and contribute to the Angular codebase and documentation

How to find more resources and tutorials

Angular has a rich and diverse ecosystem of resources and tutorials that can help you learn and improve your Angular skills. To find more resources and tutorials, you can:

- Visit the official Angular website, where you can find the official Angular documentation, guides, examples, and API reference
- Visit the official Angular learning platform, where you can find the official Angular interactive tutorial, courses, and workshops
- Visit the official Angular blog[1], where you can find the official Angular announcements, insights, and tips
- Visit the official Angular YouTube channel, where you can find the official Angular videos, tutorials, and talks
- Visit the Angular University website, where you can find high-quality Angular courses, articles, and podcasts
- Visit the Angular In Depth website, where you can find in-depth Angular articles, tutorials, and case studies
- Visit the Angular Tips website, where you can find useful Angular tips, tricks, and

snippets

How to get feedback and support

Angular has a friendly and supportive community of developers, enthusiasts, and experts who are willing to help you with your Angular projects and problems. To get feedback and support, you can:

- Join the official Angular Discord server, where you can chat, ask questions, and get feedback from other Angular developers
- Join the official Angular Gitter channel, where you can chat, ask questions, and get feedback from other Angular developers
- Join the official Angular Reddit community, where you can post, comment, and get feedback from other Angular developers
- Join the official Angular Stack Overflow community, where you can ask and answer Angular questions, and get feedback from other Angular developers
- Join the official Angular GitHub repository, where you can report issues, submit pull requests, and get feedback from the Angular team and the community

This is the end of the book. You have learned how to use Angular 17 to create modern and powerful web applications. You have also learned how to keep up with Angular updates and news, how to join the Angular community and contribute, how to find more resources and tutorials, and how to get feedback and support. We hope you enjoyed this book and found it useful and informative. Thank you for reading and happy coding!